TRANSACTIONS IN INTERNATIONAL LAND MANAGEMENT

To

Jennifer and Margit
(our long-suffering wives)

and to our families

Transactions in International Land Management
Volume 4

Edited by

ROBERT W. DIXON-GOUGH
University of East London, UK

REINFRIED MANSBERGER
Universität für Bodenkultur, Austria

Ashgate

Published by
Ashgate Publishing Limited
Gower House
Croft Road
Aldershot
Hampshire GU11 3HR
England

Ashgate Publishing Company
131 Main Street
Burlington, VT 05401-5600 USA

Ashgate website: http://www.ashgate.com

British Library Cataloguing in Publication Data
Transactions in international land management
     Vol. 4 edited by Robert W. Dixon-Gough, Reinfried
     Mansberger. - (International land management series)
     1.Land use - Management
     I.Dixon-Gough, R. W. (Robert W) II.Mansberger, Reinfried
     333.7'3

Library of Congress Control Number: 00-133623

ISBN 0 7546 1785 8

Printed in Great Britain by
Antony Rowe Ltd, Chippenham, Wiltshire

Contents

Introduction

Transactions in International Land Management in common with the (accompanying) book series has the aim of encouraging the study of the complex international and multidisciplinary issues involved in international land management, such as

- surveying and valuation of the land;
- concepts of environmental issues of sustainable land development;
- acquiring semantic data of the land;
- methodologies and a comparative analysis of current practices;
- management of the land and tools for planning and land management;
- land conservation;
- evolution of the landscape;
- regulation and legislation relating to land management;
- cultural, human and social issues of land management.

Both the book series and Transactions aim to make available to students, lecturers and practical experts, material that will focus on the various aspects of land management at a variety of levels. These will range from undergraduate teaching, the dissemination of practical applications, through to the dissemination of research.

The fundamental aim of the editors and the editorial board is to encourage and promote the study of land management in the broadest possible sense. Contributions are invited from practical experts, consultants and those involved in the teaching of the discipline. A second aim is to ensure that research findings are made available to a wider audience of interested readers and that research is integrated into current practice through its wider dissemination. The third aim is to make available studies based upon the themes of conferences.

Transactions in International Land Management owes its evolution to a very successful conference organised by Dr. Richard Bullard in January 1997. The conference was on International Land Management and was organised in conjunction with the Royal Institution of Chartered Surveyors. It attracted experts in land management from across the world. Although the initial intention was to publish the papers as the proceedings of the conference, it was subsequently considered that the edited and refereed papers could be reproduced as the first four volumes of a new series of *Transactions in International Land Management*.

Transactions will be published on an irregular basis, although it is anticipated that a minimum of two volumes per year will be produced. It is anticipated that it will become an important 'journal' in the subject field of International Land Management. There is currently no competing journal that covers the diverse aspects of this subject area. The first volume of Transactions was published at the end of 2000 and volumes 2-4 will be published during 2001/2.

The following volumes of Transactions consist of:

TILM Volume 1.

- The debate over agrarian structure in Macedonia: implications for land management. *P. Bloch, J. Melmed-Sanjak and R. Hanson.*
- Implementation of land reform in Estonia. *K.I. Leväinen.*
- GIS and the management of rural land. *J. Swindell.*
- "Let us build us a city" – the growth of a town in Zambia. *E. Mutale.*
- A comparative evaluation of land registration and agrarian reform in Austria and Great Britain. *R. Mansberger, R.W. Dixon-Gough and W. Seher.*
- Encoding expert opinion in Geo-Information Systems: a fuzzy set solution. *A.J. Brimicombe.*
- Informal land delivery and management: a case of two housing areas in Zanzibar town. *M. Veijalainen.*
- The utility of some synoptic information tools for the environmental sustainability of land management strategies in the Asian context. *A.A. Remigio.*

Since Volume 1 was prepared, there have been some minor editorial changes in the order in which certain papers will appear in subsequent volumes. The content of volumes 2 and 3 will be as follows:

TILM Volume 2.

- Contaminated land investigation and risk assessment: a case study in Portsmouth. *J. Clay and T. Viney.*
- Analysis on economic constraints to multiple-use forest management in the Amazon Region. *Z.A.G.P. da Gama e Silva, V.A. Hoeflich and L.R. Graça.*
- Was the change in land ownership necessary? *M. Rizov.*
- Riparian zones: issues of definition and management. *A. Jarvis and H. Cook.*
- Property rights revisited: institutional change and land reform: a case study of community forestry in Nepal. *S. Tiwari and F. Quinn.*
- Development of land for new urban areas: in search of a new approach. *H. de Wolff.*
- Land management in rural areas of Poland: background to the economic transformation in the nineties. *A. Muczyński, S. Surowiec and W. Zebrowski.*
- Urban land readjustment in the development process: the influence of property owners. *K. Viitanen.*
- Land management in small island states. *D. Greenwood.*
- Citizenship, society and the management of land. *N. Ravenscroft.*

TILM Volume 3.

- Implementing 'negotiated' land reform: the case of Colombia. *J. Heath.*
- Environmental management: the challenge for rural chartered surveyors. *S. Markwell and N. Ravenscroft.*
- Status and driving force of the sandy desertification in the Yarlung Zangbo river basin in the Southern Qinghai-Xizang (Tibet) Plateau. *Dong Yuxaing, Dong Guangrong and Li Sen.*
- Impact of spatial distribution of land contamination on property investment appraisal. *P.J. Kennedy, C.P. Nathanial, A. Abbachi and I.D. Martin.*
- Layout of farmland plots. *P.K. Sky.*
- Management of agricultural real properties situated within town limits. *R. Źróbek and S. Źróbek.*

- The impact of ecological demands on the process of reallotment. *A.M. Buis.*
- The Channel Tunnel rail link: land use problems in Kent. *R. Haywood.*
- Environmental impact of constructing sea defences in a coastal zone. *R.K. Bullard.*

The first two books in the series, *Land Reform and Sustainable Development and European Coastal Zone Management* were published in November, 1999 and March 2001 respectively and other forthcoming titles include:

Communal Land Ownership: Remnant of the Past?
Land Consolidation and Rural Development
Subsistence and Land Use Amongst Indigenous Peoples

If you are interested in submitting a paper for publication in the *Transactions of International Land Management*, please contact either the editors or any member of the Editorial Board.

The Editorial Board for Transactions consists of:

Dr. Peter Bloch, Land Tenure Centre, University Wisconsin-Madison
pcbloch@facstaff.wisc.edu
Fred Brazier, Ordnance Survey International Relations Manager
abrazier@ordsvy.gov.uk
Professor Allan Brimicombe, School of Surveying, University of East London
A.J.Brimicombe@uel.ac.uk
Dr. Richard Bullard, School of the Built Environment, Anglia Polytechnic University
Richard.Bullard@cwcom.org
Frank Byamugisha, World Bank, Washington
Fbyamugisha@worldbank.org
Dr. Hadrian Cook, Imperial College at Wye, University of London
H.Cook@wye.ac.uk
Dr. Peter Dare, Department of Geodesy and Geomatics, University of New Brunswick, Canada
Dare@unb.ca

With each volume of Transactions, a brief 'portrait' will be given of the members of the Editorial Board.

Dr. Peter Bloch graduated in 1974 from the University of California at Berkeley, in Economics. His PhD dissertation examined the structure of non-agricultural earnings in Brazil. He has been employed by the Land Tenure Centre, University of Wisconsin-Madison, since 1984 and recently received a teaching appointment in the same university's Department of Forest Ecology and Management.

His current research and technical advisory work is primarily divided between Central Asia, especially Kyrgyzstan, and francophone Africa, including Senegal, Mali and Chad. In Central Asia, he works on the development of real estate markets in the context of agrarian reform; in Africa he assists the Inter-state Committee for Drought Control in the Sahel in the establishment of land tenure observatories in the organisation's member countries and in studies of tenure issues in a variety of niches, including irrigated agriculture and natural resource management. He is also beginning to do work in the US, currently studying access to land by Southeast Asian immigrants who wish to farm.

Fred Brazier graduated in 1967 from the University of Newcastle upon Tyne in Land Surveying and Geography. He qualified as a Professional Associate of the Royal Institution of Chartered Surveyors in 1969 and was elected a Fellow in 1982. He joined the Directorate of Overseas Surveys in 1975, which became Ordnance Survey International (OSI) in 1992. Much of his early career was spent surveying and mapping various countries in Africa - Malawi, Nigeria, Sudan, Zambia, Kenya, Liberia, Sierra Leone, Botswana.

Since 1997 he has been managing OSI projects in the Caribbean - including the establishment of a digital map production facility in Trinidad and Tobago, Mapping Policy in Barbados, and Public Land Administration and Regularisation of Tenure in Guyana. He represented OSI throughout the Caribbean Region.

His current appointment is Ordnance Survey (OS) International Relations Manager: formulating and maintaining policy; co-ordinating and, where appropriate, representing OS interests on international organisations; managing international liaison visits to the OS; managing staff who are seconded to and from other international organisations for 'public good' reasons; and co-ordinating international conferences and events on behalf of OS.

Professor Allan Brimicombe graduated in geography from the University of Sheffield in 1976 and subsequently spent 12 years as an engineering geomorphologist with Binnie and Partners working on projects in Hong Kong, China and Malaysia. He joined Hong Kong Polytechnics in 1988 and became the founding Head of the Department of Land Surveying and Geo-Informatics. He returned to the UK in 1995 to become the first Head of the newly combined, School of Surveying at the University of East London, being awarded the Chair in 1999.

He has published extensively and his principal research interests lies in the operational aspects of GIS.

Dr. Richard K Bullard is a freelance consultant and Reader in the Department of the Built Environment at Anglia Polytechnic University (APU). His surveying career began in Zimbabwe and to date he has worked in thirty-seven countries. He completed his Masters in Engineering (by research) at the University of the Witwatersrand, Johannesburg, and his doctorate at Sheffield University. He was involved with FIG as a national delegate and as Secretary of Commission 2 (Education) and is currently a corresponding member of Commission 7 (Cadastre and Land Management). He is also involved with the RICS as an examiner and is currently a member of Geomatics Faculty Board and of the Executive. He is a member of the European Faculty of Land Use and Development and is currently a Professor in *Systemes d'Information du Territoire*. Richard has a particular interest in the multidisciplinary aspects of land development for countries in transition and in the developing world and is the author of books, chapters and publications in the above fields of activity.

He was the organiser for the 1st International Conference on Land Management in 1997 and was co-organiser for the 2nd International Conference on Land Management in 2001, for which the other series editors of the International Land Management book series formed the international organising committee for the event.

Frank Byamugisha graduated from Makerere University in 1977 with a Bachelors Degree in Agriculture (Agricultural Economics). This was followed by Masters Degrees in Agricultural Development Economics, from the Australian National University (1980), and Surveying from the University of East London (1999). Between 1980 and 1983, he worked as a Senior Economist and later Assistant Secretary for Economic Policy in the Department of Finance of the Government of Papua, New Guinea. Since September 1983, he has worked at the World Bank, where he is currently a Principal Operations Officer and Chairman of the World Bank's Land Policy and Administration Thematic Group.

His day-to-day work has largely been confined to work on land projects across East Asia and the Pacific Region. To ensure that he remains updated in other regions of the world, he has started to get involved in land-related projects in Bulgaria and market-assisted land reforms in Latin America.

Dr. Hadrian Cook is a Senior Lecturer in Hydrology. A member of the Chartered Institute of Water and Environmental Management and the British Society of Soil Science. He teaches most aspects of Hydrology and water policy together with aspects of environmental history. His main research interests are: groundwater protection policy development, soil water conservation and the management and operation of historic water management systems such as watermeadows and grazing marshes. In addition to his research publications, he has written and edited books concerned with water policy and management.

Dr. Peter Dare joined the Department of Geodesy and Geomatics Engineering at the University of New Brunswick as an Associate Professor in August 2000. Previously he had been a senior lecturer in the School of Surveying, University of East London, England His main areas of expertise are in Geodesy, GPS and Operational Research (OR) but in addition he has experience in the broad field of Geomatics. Dr Dare has used OR to help solve aspects of the GPS logistics problem - further research in this area is continuing. He is also carrying out an investigation into the status of DTMs in Canada. In addition to the more theoretical aspects of GPS, he also takes part in practical Geomatics work. For example, in 2000 he took part in an international archaeological project at a World Heritage Site in Turkmenistan. His role was to produce a base map using a combination of space imagery and GPS.

Dr Dare is a member of the American Geophysical Union and the UK Operational Research Society. He is a Fellow of the Royal Astronomical Society and a Fellow of the Royal Institution of Chartered Surveyors (RICS). He is active on committees of the RICS including the Geomatics Faculty Board. He is also a member of FIG working group, 'Reference Frames in Practice'.

Mark Deakin is a Senior Lecturer and Teaching Fellow in the School of the Built Environment, Napier University. He has also been responsible for developing under-graduate and post-graduate programmes in land and property management. The undergraduate programmes include BSc (Hons) degrees in Estate Management and Planning and Development Surveying. At post-graduate level the programmes include an MSc and MBA in Property and Construction Management.

He has carried out research into the development of land management for the past five years. The research projects in question include those on contemporary land and property management funded by the Royal Institution of Chartered Surveyors, British Know-How Fund and Overseas Development Agency. As a partner in BEQUEST (Building Environmental Quality Evaluation for Sustainability through Time), he is responsible for reviewing the assessment methods currently available for the evaluation of sustainability. This research project is funded by the European Commission. He is a regular contributor to property journals specialising in the field of management science and has recently edited a book entitled: *Local Authority Property Management: Initiatives, Strategies, Re-organisation and Reform.*

Robert Dixon-Gough has been a member of staff of the School of Surveying since 1974 and is currently a Senior Lecturer. Previously, he was a cartographer who specialised in water resource planning. He became actively interested in remote sensing in 1980 and co-authored *Britain from Space* in 1985. His main research interests are: practical applications of remote sensing, particularly in the field of coastal zone management and assessing land cover changes; laand management effects upon coastal regions; land information systems for the purpose of land registration and land reform; land and environmental conservation, and rural land use and planning. He is also the UK representative on the management committee of the EU COST G9 exercises, Modelling Real Esate Transactions.

Mr Dixon-Gough is an elected member of the European Faculty of Land Use and Development, Strasbourg and has been appointed Professeur Extroirdinaire of that organisation. His affiliations include the European Union of Coastal Conservation and the Remote Sensing Society. He has published extensively in his areas of research interests. He was co-organiser for the 2nd International Conference on Land Management in 2001.

Roger Fisher graduated in Mining Engineering from Imperial College, London in 1958 and in Land Surveying from the University of Cape Town in 1972. In 1980 he took the MPhil degree at the University of Cambridge. During an academic career of some 30 years he has specialised in cadastre and land law. He has been Head of Department of Surveying at the University of Cape Town and at North East London Polytechnic (now the University of East London) and most recently Dean of Faculty at the latter university. His main research interests have been in the fields of boundary law and land rights with a particular interest in Southern Africa. Since 1998 he has operated his own surveying consultancy practice.

Dr. Robert Home is a Reader in Planning at the University of East London and holds degrees from Cambridge University, the London School of Economics and Oxford Brookes University. He teaches most aspects of town planning with emphasis upon developing countries. His main research areas are planning regulations, planning history and land management. He has published widely on planning practice and undertaken research and consultancy work in Nigeria, Malaysia, China, Bulgaria, Pakistan and South Africa.

Professor Crispus Kiamba is an Associate Professor in the Department of Land Development, University of Nairobi, Kenya. He holds a BA in Land Economics from the University of Nairobi, a MSc in Land Appraisal from the University of Reading and a PhD from the University of Cambridge. He is presently on leave from the Department of Land Development as the Deputy Vice-Chancellor in charge of Administration and Finance of the University of Nairobi. He has previously been the Principal of the College of Architecture and Engineering and the Dean of the Faculty of Architecture, Design and Development of the same University.

Professor Kiamba has main research interests in urban issues, land management and environmental and development issues. He is a Member of the Institution of Surveyors of Kenya. He has also been a Member of the Bureau of the International Federation for Housing and Planning and a Member of the Rural and Urban Planners in Southern and Eastern Africa.

Dr. Reinfried Mansberger graduated from the Technical University in Vienna in Geodesy having majored in photogrammetry and Cartography. His PhD thesis was on developing a system for semi-automatic interpretation of tree crown conditions using colour infrared aerial photographs. Between 1983 and 1987, he was appointed as a university assistant at the Institute of Applied Geodesy and Photogrammetry at the Technical University at Graz before being appointed as a research assistant at the Institute of Surveying, Remote Sensing and Land Information, Universität für Bodenkultur Wien (University of Agricultural Sciences, Vienna). He is currently Assistant Professor at this institute.

Dr Mansberger is the Austrian correspondent of Commission VII (Resource and Environmental Monitoring) of the International Society of Photogrammetry and Remote Sensing. He is also actively involved in the International Federation of Surveyors as a correspondent member and webmaster of Commission 3 (Spatial Data Management) and is an elected member of the European Faculty of Land Use and Development. His principal research interests are: Land Use Planning, Land Information, Photogrammetry, Environmental GIS Applications, and Cadastral Systems.

Dr. Walter Seher graduated in 1994 from the Universität für Bodenkultur Wien (University of Agricultural Sciences, Vienna), in Rural Engineering and Water Management. He is currently appointed as a Lecturer in this university at the Institute of Regional Planning and Rural Development.

He has recently been involved in research projects concerning: the cultivation of alpine meadows and the implementation of Alpine National Parks in Austria; a comparative evaluation of three agri-environmental programmes in France, Germany and Austria; mobile flood protection elements; and the impacts of set-aside vineyards on cultivation, ecology, landscape image and the development of settlement structures in Lower Austria. His special fields of interest are: rural development, land consolidation, agri-environmental programmes, agriculture and nature conservation, and land use planning and water management (especially flood protection).

Dr. Per Kåre Sky graduated with a Masters degree from the Agricultural University of Norway in 1989 with academic specialisations in surveying, mapping, cadastre and land consolidation. That same university awarded him his PhD in 1995. His post graduate studies have taken him to the Universities of Aalborg (Denmark) and Oslo (Norway).

After graduating, Dr Per Kåre Sky worked until 1995 as a Senior Engineer/Head of Section for Land Information Systems and Land Use Planning for the Property Division of the Norwegian Defence Construction Service. He was appointed to the position of Associate Researcher/Associate Professor of the Department of Land Use and Landscape Planning, Agricultural University of Norway in 1994. He is now the Professor in Land Consolidation at that university, a part-time position that allows him also to act as a Land Consolidation Judge for the Land Consolidation Court of Nord- and Midhorland. Dr Per Kåre Sky is also the Regional Director of Land Consolidation Services for the County of Hordaland.

His research interests includes the use of GIS in the land re-adjustment process, the use of GIS-based analytical tools, developed to assist the economic analyses of different physical layout of farmland plots, land consolidation in Cyprus, and mediation in the land consolidation courts of Norway.

Dr Per Kåre Sky is an Honorary Fellow at the Institute of Legal Studies at the University of Wisconsin-Madison and has made several study tours to the Land Consolidation Department in Cyprus. In 2000, he was appointed as Editor-in-Chief of the Norwegian Journal of Mapping and Planning Services.

Herman de Wolff graduated in 1988 from Delft University of Technology, in Geodetic Engineering, with an additional certificate in Systems Engineering, Policy Analysis and Management. From 1987 to 1988 he worked as a researcher for the Chamber of Commerce in the field of urban renewal. After graduating, he worked at a research assistant/non-tenured lecturer at Delft University of Technology. Since 1992 he has been working as assistant professor/lecturer for the section Geo-information and Land Development of de Department of Geodesy. Herman de Wolff has been the secretary of the working group POLIS, since 1998. This is an association of Dutch Geodetic Engineers working in the field of urban and rural land development.

His main area of expertise is urban development. Within this interdisciplinary field, his research and teaching activities are focussed on plan implementation strategies and governmental instruments for land development in new urban areas, urban regeneration and public-private co-operation in urban development projects. His research is mainly from the perspective of legal, public administration and organisation, and includes both scientific research and consultancy projects for central government and municipalities. Recently, he was responsible for the research for the governmental assessment of the Dutch Pre-emption Act.

Robert Dixon-Gough and Reinfried Mansberger

Serving without land: the Grameen way

Dr. Mohammad MOMEN
Bangladesh Public Administration Training Centre, Savar, Dhaka, Bangladesh

Abstract

The number of potential claimants for land in Bangladesh far exceeds the supply. The continual displacement of labour from agriculture and the incapacity of the industrial sector to gainfully employ the surplus labour have aggravated the situation of poverty, unemployment, and landlessness in the countryside. Land redistribution programme has failed, and does not appear implementable because of the structural dependence of the state on the rural elite and bureaucrats. The analysis of four decades of attempted land reform and rural development suggests that all state sponsored development interventions in the countryside have virtually bypassed the landless. Against this background Grameen Bank has been claimed as a successful innovative institution with considerable relief for the landless, without confronting the state or disturbing the prevailing social order. This paper interprets Grameen as a model, which serves the landless more effectively than any other land contingent programme. With extreme land scarcity and limited scope for agricultural expansion, the equitable distribution of land among ten million landless rural families does not seem practical. This paper suggests that serving the landless with available alternative tool, for example, with that of micro-credit operation and management of Grameen would be a pragmatic approach in addressing the problems of landlessness and rural poverty.

Introduction

From the agrarian point of view, despite being known to be one of the richest agricultural bases on the planet (Hartmann and Boyce, 1981), Bangladesh has one of the world's hungriest populations (Prosterman *et al*, 1990) to feed depending on no more than 0.07 hectare of *per capita* cultivable land (Momen, 1996). The scenario of Bangladesh, measured through the World Bank's matrix of development is encouraging (World Bank, 1996). Offsetting the impressive rise in the production of food grain and modest swelling in *per capita* GNP (the question of *per capita* real income, however, remains little mentioned) the population below the poverty line expanded quickly, while persistent hunger and under nutrition in the countryside continued to be a major concern. During the 1980s and 1990s, land reforms staged a comeback in the transitional economies, but for the others the advocacy of as well as need for land reform seems to have declined, with the shift of agenda to other pressing issues such as market, environment and gender issues. With more than half of the rural households in Bangladesh being landless, lying below the poverty line, and having a limited prospect for land reform, it is essential to search for viable alternatives. The country plunged into famine in 1974 and famine-like situation re-surfaced several times during the following years. It is estimated that during the famine of 1974, four million metric tons of rice were available but the starving people were 'too poor to buy' (Raymer, 1975, quoted in Lappe *et al*, 1977:19). Bangladesh, being a land-poor country, encounters the growing trend of landlessness in the face of a growing population on the one hand, and poverty and unemployment on the other. Landlessness by the 1990s had affected nearly 60% of the population in the countryside.

The state in Bangladesh, like many other post-colonial countries, may be seen as a military-bureaucratic oligarchy, with politicians as the third partner in the coalition (Alavi, 1973). The overall ruling elite, as in many other Asian countries is composed of, or structurally or electorally dependent on, the agrarian elite (Herring, 1983). The distorted application of such measures during the period between 1950-94 has reduced tenure, increased landlessness, and contributed to the process of manipulating existing institutions in favour of the ruling elite (Wood, 1994). It has been evidenced that land reform benefited the non-cultivating refugees in the 1950s, soldiers in the 1960s and political elite in the 1970s, while the landless gained little from the state-sponsored programmes. With the President of the country delaying the issuance of land ceiling laws to protect his own land through transfer-adjustment, and the landed elite applying similar tactics, there was little available land for the landless (Momen, 1996).

In the 1990s, the attention was on micro credit. For the land-poor countries, credit has long been envisaged as a gateway to income, but institutional sources developed on the ethics of banking, bypassed the collateral-poor landless. The public sector intervention in the imperfect credit market was invited to impose low ceilings on interest rates, allocate credit to yield rural development, and rationalise income distribution (Braverman and Gausch, 1993). Experience has suggested that the benefits of state intervention and subsidised credit have largely been monopolised by medium and large landholders. With a growing population, together with urban expansion, military installation, and the incremental use of farmland for various non-agricultural purposes (Bullard, 1993), *per capita* arable land by the first quarter of the 21st century will be about 0.04 hectare, which may seriously affect the agrarian population. Estimates, even ambitious ones, do not project Bangladesh as a nation independent of food imports. Even if food self-sufficiency is attained, it does not assure food security in the countryside. In this situation, a sustainable income is more important than the possession of land.

Land reform and rural development

A good law, by itself, does not necessarily guarantee an effective implementation. The Act of 1950, once hailed as the 'Magna Carta of the Bengal peasants', was implemented in a way that only succeeded in generated further misery for the small, marginal, and landless peasants. Although all the Five Year Plans contained the rhetoric of land reform and even though the socialist transformation of society sometime emerged as a national priority, the land system remained the same, relatively inefficient, exploitative, and practically unreformed. Rural development in Bangladesh was never seriously taken as an anti-poverty measure. The famous Comilla Approach seemed to be a 'viable answer to the quest for rural development' (Blair, 1978:65), was latter criticised for bettering the rural rich and dragging the poor down to further impoverishment. The government-sponsored rural development programmes in Bangladesh may be characterised by the following:

- rural development programmes and projects dependent upon the external funds;
- new programmes, apparently paved with good intention aimed at legitimising non-democratic governments by distributing undue benefits;
- operational mechanisms of state-owned, rural development that excluded the landless from the benefits of the distribution network;
- at an early stage, funds were diverted towards the development of the urban infrastructure;

- some of the experiments succeeded as pilot projects but failed when replicated elsewhere;
- elite dependent programmes failed to mobilise local resources, organise the beneficiaries, and ensure their participation;
- the expansion of employment opportunities was minimal;
- rural initiatives succumbed to the control-oriented central bureaucracy.

The genesis of Grameen

Professor Mohammed Yunus, while teaching his students economics in the post-independent Bangladesh at the University of Chittagong, had a realisation that the brilliant theories of economics he was teaching were of no practical use in attacking hunger and starvation (Yunus, 1994a). When the country plunged into famine during 1974, he left the textbook and confronted the economy of real life, fraught with hunger, and poverty and indebtedness. He met a landless poor woman, who had the survival skill and was a hard worker, yet could not earn more than 2 cents (US) a day in her desperate effort to survive with the members of her family. Making bamboo stools could not raise her daily income above 2 cents, because she could not amass a modest working capital of 20 cents to buy raw materials. A village trader lent her a conditional capital, which never allowed her take-home money of more than 2 cents a day. Yunus assembled 42 persons who had no material resources or working capital, and were trapped in a vicious circle of debt. He wanted to free them from the moneylenders, and estimated that an initial working capital of US $30 would be required to support their economic activities. He lent that amount to 42 persons representing 42 rural landless families. The immediate solution to their problem was not very difficult, and did not demand a rigorous exercise of economic theories, but it was not a sustainable solution. He attempted to establish a link between a local bank and his clients, but failed on the very legitimate banking grounds that his clients were too poor to provide land or any other valuables as collateral against the monetary value of loan. He was mocked for not being able to understand the banking ethics.

The professor, however, did not give up his attempt to establish an institutional linkage, which he viewed as the very first step in addressing the problems of his clients. He assumed that with access to credit on reasonable terms and conditions, the rural poor would be able to generate income and employment. With him standing as guarantor for any default of payment, he finally, persuaded a bank to agree to give him money to lend to the poor. Within months, his assumption was proved to be valid. He was able to show that lending to the poor without collateral was no riskier than lending to the rich against collateral. Based on this finding concerning the strength of credit, the following objectives were framed:

- extend banking facilities to the rural poor;
- eliminate the exploitation by money-lenders;
- create opportunity for self-employment;
- bring the disadvantaged people into an organisational format which they can understand and operate;
- reverse the vicious circle of 'low income, low saving, low investment'.

The actions of the research project were considered to be a success. The striking discovery was that the poor were highly bankable, and had an excellent sense of the efficient use of credit. While the bankers were yet to be convinced, he continued to lend to the poor in greater numbers, throughout larger areas, and found that the system worked. The poor clients did not default. The central bank (Bangladesh Bank) was convinced that the poor might be bankable with Yunus as the manager. The credit recovery was not yet enough to convince bank officials to open a till in their banks for the poor and asset-less people. He eventually decided to establish a bank for the poor. The Grameen Bank (*Grameen* literally means rural) was established in 1983 as an institution that lends money to the poor who have no collateral. Grameen has now extended its services to more than 2 million landless families in 35,000 villages throughout rural Bangladesh.

Credit for the landless poor

The rural poor peoples' chances to bring about changes in their lives are constrained by several factors, namely the lack of access to resources, the lack of their own organisations, dominance of local money-lenders and traders, and the dependent and marginalised nature of their lives (Oakley and Marsden, 1990). Subsidised rural credit has long been envisaged as an effective attack on low productivity and rural poverty (Braverman and Gausch, 1986). However, as the result of serious imperfections in the rural credit market, government intervention was considered necessary to regulate it to benefit the perennially deprived poor and small holders.

The agrarian structure of the country and the dominance of the landed class in the credit market, have always restricted the access of institutional credit to poor peoples. Banks demand land as collateral, a common mechanism applied to deny the landless access to the formal credit markets. Even small and marginal farmers owning small areas of land do not approach a bank. They have discovered, through experience, that a bank lends to the rich alone so their only opportunity of acquiring a loan is through the usurious credit market. The experience of the past four decades in the developing countries of Asia, suggests that the establishment of institutional alternatives (rural banks and credit co-operatives) did not drive usurers out of the market (Hoff and Stiglitz, 1993). The bank officials are in favour of big loans rather than numerous small ones, and have a 'deeply entrenched attitudinal bias' towards bigger landholders (Ahluwalia, 1990:113).

The conventional wisdom, which has developed around poverty and credit, contains a bias against the poor and assumes that the poor are not credit worthy. Yunus (1993) envisaged credit as a powerful weapon to create an entitlement to resources and believed that credit without discipline becomes charity, which ultimately destroys the ability of the poor. He was critical of the global credit operation based on collateral, which excluded the poor from the financial institutions. He noted that:

> if collateral alone can provide the basis for the banking business, the society should, without any hesitation, mark out the banks as the harmful engines for creating economic, social and political inequality by making the rich richer and poor poorer (Yunus, 1993:11).

Participation of the clients

Grameen works among the population in the lowest rung of the social and economic structure. This bypassed agricultural population provides the bulk of agricultural labour, but agriculture does not consume more than a fifth of their time available for labour (*ibid.*). During the field research in 1994, the author found that 65.0% of the beneficiaries had no land at all, and 95.0% had none or less than 0.20 hectare. Grameen envisaged credit as a fundamental human right. Yunus (1994) advanced the proposition that access to credit gave the poor a chance to improve their lives and create self-employment for both

6

men and women, almost instantaneously. The creation of wage employment is not seen as a proven and happy road towards the reduction of poverty:

> Employment *per se* does not remove poverty; rather improper design of employment can turn into a mechanism, which might further accentuate poverty (Yunus, 1993:13).

The Grameen approach to credit is that of making it a weapon to create an entitlement to resources. Where macro-economic policies have failed to attack poverty, Grameen offers a micro-level solution (Shams, 1992) in a credit market infested with the problems of asymmetric information and imperfect enforcement (Khandaker *et al*, 1994). Although default is a significant aspect of the institutional credit market, Grameen shows that participative management eliminates such risk. Grameen sends out the bank workers at branch level to form five-member groups of landless people of similar economic standing, who elect their chair and a secretary for one year. All the members become the chair and secretary by rotation as a part of process of learning through experience. The bank sanctions loans to the individuals, but holds the group responsible for any default amongst its members. Fuglesang and Chandler (1988) discovered that the group members interact in a micro-network of mutual accountabilities, resulting in the creation of a dependable social collateral. They argue that the spatial and social closeness of the members lead to the creation of a well-functioning, cohesive group, with all individuals kept in line by peer pressure, and sustained support from the group. Stiglitz (1993) focused on the peer monitoring by Grameen as an effective incentive-monitoring system, and suggested that the denial of further credit to the defaulting group acts as a powerful incentive device. Peer pressure, although not a particularly new concept, has revived in the global micro-credit market after the success of Grameen. Jain (1996:80), however, maintains that the core innovation of the bank is not the collective responsibility for loan repayment:

> but fostering a combination of strategic credit policy and credit conducive culture among employees and clients.

Between 5 and 8 Grameen groups within a neighbourhood arrange weekly meetings in a place called the 'centre', with a centre-chief and a deputy centre-chief elected from among the members. The local branch of the Grameen attends the centre on the meeting day to realise repayable credit instalments and to disburse the subsequent credits. The centre-chief ensures that the overall discipline, according to the laws and by-laws of Grameen, which includes ensuring the attendance of members and the repayment of weekly instalments. Credit is advanced without collateral, since the individual, group, and bank workers represent collective social collateral, which replaces the material collateral (Fuglesang and Chandler, 1988). Members of the group operate the group fund and this process promotes the spirit and technique of the collective management of their finances (Wahid, 1993). Transparency in credit transaction is a prominent feature of the Grameen operation and Khandaker *et al* (1994) found the operational transparency to be a major instrument of its success. All transactions are made at an open meeting in the centre. Everything from investment to marketing is discussed during the meeting and all decisions (including awarding a member penalty for material or moral default) are taken by consensus. Grameen thrusts the responsibility of its ownership to the members. Each member has to purchase a Grameen share of Tk 100 (US $2.50 in 1994), which makes him a sharer and gives him feeling of ownership. Mobilisation of savings is an integral credit condition. Every week the each member of the group deposits Tk 1.00 (2.50 cents) to form a group fund, which is operated by the group and provides the members with a 'little bank', helping the members to escape starvation, avoid the rural money lenders and even providing for quick supplementary investment. During the study conducted during 1994, it was found that the small savings of Tk 1.00 a week had mounted to a huge amount of Tk 11.20 million (US $280,000) in an old Grameen branch. The creditors pay a mandatory insurance premium to cover emergency situations such as involuntary default, accidental disability, death, natural disasters, etc.

Promoting the socio-economic status of the clients

Conventional wisdom focuses on the ignorance, vices, incapacity, apathy, lethargy, and irrationality of poor people in the management of economic problems, which fill the notebooks of the rural development researchers. Grameen discards such pessimistic wisdom and views the rural poor as the engine of growth (Yunus, 1994b). The long-term solution to the problems of acute poverty lies in the generation of employment (Ahluwalia, 1990). By 1992, Grameen had advanced loans for approximately 450 various activities. Some of those activities, within the broader category of processing and manufacturing, indicate the diversity and expansion of their knowledge, skill and aptitude, and includes bamboo, cane and pottery products, the preparation

8

of snacks, puffed rice, syrup, papadum, purified butter, cold drinks, furniture, rope, cosmetics, utensils, mosquito coils, garments, handloom goods, embroidered quilts, sanitary goods, bicycle repairs, rickshaws, shoes, watches and clocks, welding, oil crushing, painting, printing, etc.. Grameen did not dictate the client's economic decisions, since they decided their own course of action through inter and intra-group meetings and discussions. Grameen offered loans for collective enterprises, ranging from Tk 50,000 to Tk 500,000, for leasing land for joint cultivation, purchase of power tillers and shallow tube-wells for irrigation, establishing oil crushing and rice husking mills and initiating any larger venture in the farm and non-farm sectors. Loans in the collective enterprises are issued against the centre, but the members equally share the repayment of loans.

Table 1 Value of assets of the client before and after joining Grameen

Value of Assets	Pre-Grameen Period		Post-Grameen Assets	
Tk	Number of households	Percentage of households	Number of households	Percentage of households
0- 1,000	6	30.0	-	-
1,001-5,000	7	35.0	2	10.0
5,001-10,000	5	25.0	4	20.0
10,001-20,000	2	10.0	4	20.0
20,001-50,000	-	-	3	15.0
50,001-100,000	-	-	5	25.0
>100,000	-	-	2	10.0
	20	100.0	20	100.0

Source: Field study by the Author.

The field research attempted to assess the economic impact of Grameen in terms of the expansion/reduction of the total assets. A total of 20 Grameen borrowers (14 female and 6 male) associated with Grameen for periods ranging from 4 to 10 years were studied. Their pre-Grameen and post-Grameen assets were valued at current market prices. The study found an impressive rise in the assets position of Grameen clients. The borrowers attributed the rise in their family income primarily to two factors: being free of moneylenders, and having widened scope for participation in a range of economic activities. All the 20 Grameen respondents in the study had borrowed from the informal lenders, 65% (13) on usurious terms with 20% (4) of them failing to recover their mortgaged assets. Interest paid to usurers ranged from 60% to 180%. Some 20% (4) of Grameen borrowers still borrow from their friends and relatives to supplement their investment or consumption needs, but moneylenders are no longer used. One female borrower, a new entrant in Grameen, had yet to clear her outstanding debt to the moneylenders, but had reduced the debt burden considerably. Although it is difficult to assess the impact of Grameen on the usurious lending market, in the absence of reliable data, Ghai (1984), Rahman (1986), Roy (1987), and Todd (1996) suggested a rapid displacement of high interest lending of the former moneylenders by Grameen. Another aspect of the Grameen intervention is the massive reduction in unproductive expenditures, such as dowries and other social obligations among its clients. Loans received for productive investment leaves little scope for consumption due to peer pressure and the compulsion to pay regular instalments. Table 1 illustrates the changes in the value of material possessions of Grameen members.

The study considers the Tk 0-5,000 assets group to be extremely poor, Tk 5,001-50,000 poor, and those in the Tk 50,001 and above, not to be poor. Table 1 reveals that 35% of Grameen households have come out of poverty. The percentage of extremely poor households had been reduced from 65% to 10%, which by any standard is an impressive achievement. A BIDS survey on Grameen suggested that it had improved the economic condition of 91.2% of client families (Rahman, 1993). Those studies, including that of the author, witnessed that Grameen had considerably widened the economic horizon of the poor and destitute.

Grameen's focus on women

In developing countries, women and rural poverty are inter-woven in various ways. The interacting effects of intra-household and societal gender inequities give women less access to all basic necessities (Safilon-Rothschild, 1991). The majority of states appear to promote a socio-economic and ideological order, which perpetuates the subordination of women, although the market treats women as individuals in their own right (Elson, 1991). With common barriers shared with men that restrict their access to credit, women are further obstructed by a number of gender-specific barriers. For example, the almost universal lack of collateral, institutional linkages, and persistent interference of male counterparts in their business, furthers the gender-stereotypic belief

10

that women cannot handle serious matters such as money, or engage in productive and profitable employment (*ibid.*). In Bangladesh, women have poor access to food, education and health, and they experience poverty differently and disproportionately (Kabeer, 1989). Despite various socio-economic constraints on the access by women to resources in Bangladesh, they have gained an 'international reputation' for their excellent credit performance in specialised credit institutions (Goetz and Gupta, 1996: 45).

Grameen began its programme in the context of a nominal 4.2% female participation in economic activities throughout the rural areas (Hossain, 1984). It focused on the women who were exploited within their family yet belonging to families that are also socially exploited. Traditionally, women had very limited access to land and other resources. Land inheritance in Bangladesh is patrilineal and *purdah* (veil, the seclusion of women) practices are prevalent. Grameen has attacked the veil-barrier without directly confronting the conservative social structure. In 1980, women constituted 39% of the borrowers, and by 1992 the percentage of male clients fell from 61% to 4%. In 1988, 96% of borrowers were women, receiving 84% of the total loan. Between 1985-92, the number of female borrowers increased by 1,205% compared with a 67% growth in the number of males. By 1992, 87.3% of loans were disbursed to females.

Grameen loans helped poor rural women to break down the gender barriers and thrust them into a market, which absorbed their products and labour. Access to markets as producers as well as labourers gave them further access to cash income, lessening their dependence on men, enhancing their economic values, increasing their powers of bargaining within and outside the households, and giving them greater dignity (Elson, 1991). Hossain (1984) suggested that before joining Grameen, 65.3% of female members had no economic occupation and no income. Credit involved them instantly in economic activities, and thereby, conferred them with status in a male dominant society.

In three economic sectors, trade, cottage industry, and livestock, women earned higher incomes than the male borrowers. Female clients spent more on education, housing, and health than their male counterparts. They were more methodical and responsive to the banking discipline and demonstrated a higher productivity per unit of loan, higher savings, and were prompter in reinvesting their surplus in productive activities (Rahman, 1986; Hossain, 1987). It is the income of the women that brings them dignity, makes them aware of their needs and rights, enlarges their choices and frees them from the traditional bondage. Rahman *et al* (1993) explained how women were placed at the core of the Grameen approach. They showed that women were quicker in responding to their economic needs and those of their children, the acceptance of contraceptives, abolition of social vices such as dowries, and to multiple marriages. Children of Grameen mothers attained a 1.4% increase in height and a 3.3% increase in weight compared to the mean national height and weight, while children belonging to the non-Grameen mothers were 0.6% below the mean national height and 6.2% below the mean national weight (calculated from Gibbons, 1994).

Using some operational measures (mobility, economic security, ability to make small and large purchase, involvement in household decisions, relative freedom within the family, political and legal awareness and involvement in political campaigning and protests) Hashemi *et al* (1996) showed that the Grameen women are more empowered than the beneficiaries of the other successful non-state programme (Bangladesh Rural Advancement Committee). It appears that they also derive higher returns from the investment of their credit.

Grameen is not a programme for empowerment, yet it appears to be more effective than the programmes that:

> profess to combat gender inequality more directly, both in its demonstrated ability to reach poor women in large numbers, and it its potential to empower women (*ibid.*: 561).

In a survey (Goetz and Gupta, 1996) suggested, however, that in gender specific credit programmes women often lose control over the credit as the credit is often invested by their male relatives. But compared with the beneficiaries of the other credit institutions, Grameen women have succeeded in retaining a higher level of control over both credit and output. It has also been identified that being unable to make informed assessment of market condition, women will loose 'control over a critical phase of production process' (*ibid.*: 59).

Is Grameen a successful rural financial institution?

The success of a bank, particularly that of a rural financial institution (RFI), should be viewed in terms of self-sustainability and outreach. Yaron (1994) set the following measures as indicators of financial self-sustainability:

- positive lending rate, high enough to maintain the value of equity in real terms;
- high rate of loan recovery;
- high rate of interest for deposits so that voluntary savings become significant in financing the loan portfolio;
- RFIs should have the economic capacity to maintain various administrative costs.

The outreach criteria has to be assessed on the basis of the value and number of loans, value and number of saving accounts, type of financial services offered, percentage of the rural population served, real growth of assets over a number of years, and the participation of women as clients (*ibid.*). Yaron compared Grameen with three other successful RFIs, namely the Bank of Agriculture and Agricultural Co-operative (BAAC) in Thailand, the Badan Kredit Kecamatan (BKK) and Bank Rakyat Indonesia Unit Desa (BUD) in Indonesia, all applying positive interest rates. Grameen tops them in terms of loan recovery. The savings of its clients is estimated at 31% of the loan portfolio, higher than BKK but lower than BAAC and BUD. Considering the relatively poor economic base of Grameen clients, the achievement in mobilising savings was highly commended by thee World Bank (1989). Grameen's administrative costs have increased in recent years due to a rapid growth of the number of branches. During 1986-89 it retained a real growth rate of 34%, while BKK and BAAC achieved 15% and 4%, respectively, and BUD 36%. Of these four RFIs, the Grameen reaches more of the poor in rural areas and performs a wide range of non-financial activities. It tops the list in the coverage of the rural poor (17.2% in 1986 as against 1.8% for BKK in 1989), and the participation by women. 91% of the Grameen borrowers are women (during Yaron's examination), while women account for 25% of the borrowers of BUD and 60% of BKK. The World Bank (1989) considers Grameen to be an effective approach to non-corporate finance for rural Bangladesh, and attributes its success to factors such as the close supervision of field operations, dedicated bank-workers, purpose-based borrowings for generating income, solidarity within the group and the assurance of the availability of a future loan.

Within an eleven year period, the number of Grameen borrowers increased by 1200%; from 170,000 in 1985 to 2 million in 1996, when about half of the villages in Bangladesh came under Grameen operation. The average lending per branch increased from Tk 1.86 million in 1986 to Tk 6.27 million in 1992. Grameen started its initial operation with subsidised funding through the Bangladesh Bank and IFAD. It subsequently received funds at a subsidised rate from the Dutch, Norwegian and Swedish aid agencies and the Ford Foundation. In a publication of the World Bank (Khandaker *et al*, 1994) it was suggested that in order to eliminate subsidy dependency, Grameen should double either its lending rate or annual disbursement per branch. The factors contributing to its success include decentralised operational structure, efficient monitoring and evaluation, and through a structured learning process based on trial and error with continuous fine-tuning.

The target group approach of Grameen became a countervailing force against the power elite, who sought to dominate and control inputs and which services delivery institutions (Rahman, 1986). Grameen has proved its potential as a rural bank for sustainability. With reference to the loan recovery portfolio of the Agricultural Bank (30%) and the Industrial Bank (10%) and Grameen (98%), Yunus (1994) rightly suggests that Grameen is a bank in its totality, while the two others look like charity outlets for the rich. Grameen credit drew its clients from the informal usurious lending market, not seriously affecting the moneylenders, who were found to have transferred their capital to the large rural enterprises. Quasem (1990) suggested that moneylenders in Grameen villages have channelled their money towards the establishment of brickfields, rice mills and irrigation.

Grameen and other programmes

While working among the landless, Yunus tried to establish the virtues of landlessness and credit in a Grameen situation. All Grameen members, being landless, were found to be desperate to find an alternative livelihood, enterprising, mobile, and receptive to new ideas and technology. They were free from the traditional life-style of the land-owning peasants, who sustain a 'conservative and fatalistic attitude towards life' (Yunus, 1982). Access to resources initiated changes to the socio-economic life of the poor and landless. However, the intensity of mobilisation and the extent of change depended on the nature of the organisations, on their utilisation of the packages available to them, and the market response. Four sets of beneficiaries have been studied:

- recipients of public land under land distribution programme;
- beneficiaries under the Bangladesh Rural Development Board (BRDB);

- settlers in the Cluster Villages who received a homestead, land, and a small income generating incentive;
- Grameen clients.

It was not possible to find a location where all the four programmes were in operation. Accepting the regional variation in terms of agricultural productivity and occupational pattern, data was collected from Mymensingh and Comilla, and the total family assets of the beneficiaries were assessed. 20 beneficiaries under land distribution programme received an average of 0.26 hectare of agricultural land, and each of 20 beneficiaries under the Cluster Village received 0.02 hectare of homestead land and a small tin-shed house. The BRDB beneficiaries had not benefited from the land reform programme. Table 2 gives a comparative account of economic performance of the beneficiaries under the above four programmes.

Table 2 Value of assets of the beneficiaries under four different programmes

Value of Assets	Land Distribution		BRDB		Cluster Village		Grameen Bank	
(Taka)	Pre	Post	Pre	Post	Pre	Post	Pre	Post
0-1,000	2 (10.0)	1 (5.0)	2 (10.0)	1 (5.0)	4 (20.0)	-	6 (30.0)	-
1,001-5,000	6 (30.0)	5 (25.0)	7 (35.0)	4 (20.0)	6 (30.0)	6 (30.0)	7 (35.0)	2 (10.0)
5,001-10,001	7 (35.0)	5 (25.0)	5 (25.0)	7 (35.0)	6 (30.0)	7 (35.0)	5 (25.0)	4 (20.0)
10,001-20,000	5 (25.0)	6 (30.0)	3 (15.0)	3 (15.0)	4 (20.0)	3 (15.0)	2 (10.0)	4 (20.0)
20,001-50,000	2 (10.0)	3 (15.0)	3 (15.0)	5 (25.0)	-	2 (10.0)	-	3 (15.0)
50,001-100,000	-	1 (5.0)	-	-	-	2 (10.0)	-	5 (25.0)
>100,000	-	-	-	-	-	-	-	2 (10.0)

Source: Field Study by the Author.

The assets of the beneficiaries prior to the programme and values of all assets after the programme intervention except those of land transferred under land distribution and CV, were valued at 1994 prices. All savings and the value of purchased shares were added, and loans drawn from formal and informal sources were deducted. The study considered the Tk 0-5,000 asset group to be extremely poor, Tk 5,001-50,000 poor, and Tk 50,001 and above, not to be poor. The findings of 20 respondents from each of the above four programmes suggest that 5% of beneficiaries under the land distribution programme came out of poverty, none for the BRDB, 10% for the Cluster Village (CV) and 35% for the Grameen.

Table 3 Land possession of different beneficiaries before and after the programmes

Programme	Previously owned (ha)	Received (ha)	Purchase (+)/Sale(-)	Mortgage (+)/(-)	Change in percentage *
Land Distribution	1.54	5.30	-0.64	+0.22	-27.3
BRDB	0.83	-	-	+0.24	+28.9
Cluster Village	0.71	0.50	+0.12	+0.30	+69.2
Grameen Bank	0.55	-	+0.79	+0.43	+221.8

Source: Field Study by the Author.
Note: *Increase/decrease as percentage of previously owned land.

The extremely poor households decreased from 40% to 30% under the land distribution programme, from 45% to 25% under the BRDB, 50% to 30% under the CVs and from 65% to 10% under Grameen. It suggested that the BRDB and land distribution programme had marginally succeeded in promoting the economy of a small section of the beneficiaries, CVs a modest success, while Grameen's success was impressive. Grameen's success lies in the rational utilisation of credit in non-farm activities, which generated quick income. The data on the ownership and mortgage of the land of these beneficiaries was obtained to show changes in the possession of land before and after the interventions of the concerned programmes.

The data clearly suggested that Grameen had provided higher access to land, while land distribution (except for the distributed land) failed to promote further access to land. Compared with the BRDB, Grameen's success is 8 times higher in terms of promoting the clients' possession of land.

A critic of Grameen

Grameen has been confronted by a range of criticism (Hossain, 1984; Osmani, 1989; Yaron, 1993; Siamwalla, 1993; Rahman, 1993). Some of those criticisms are summarised below:

- although Grameen has been a success in the short term, it cannot be sustained without being integrated within the local level planning;
- markets have not expanded enough to absorb the output of the Grameen beneficiaries;
- it cannot cover all the existing and potential poor in a locality, and thus will allow the problems of poverty to continue;
- the expansion of Grameen will not contribute to economic growth, as it will fail to mobilise capital due to poor ability of people to save, and will contribute towards inflation in the economy by increasing demands for consumer goods;
- some Grameen projects have recorded lower productivity than agricultural wages;
- slow growth in agriculture will impose structural constraints on its expansion and profitable operation;
- it cannot make any significant progress in addressing the issue of poverty in the existing iniquitous structure, while it remains a marginal institution;
- it has promoted trading, not manufacturing;
- withdrawal of subsidised funding will destabilise Grameen;
- the borrowers have developed a propensity to invest in land;
- Grameen is a highly management-intensive institution. Institutional rigidity and lack of promotion opportunities will hamper its long-term efficiency;
- increases in the size of individual loans will stimulate corrupt practices;
- the absence of its charismatic founder will affect the performance of the bank.

Although many of these criticisms cannot be substantiated in a statistical manner, the failures of many other rural development and poverty alleviation programmes provides some doubts concerning the sustainability of Grameen.

Its success has lowered the cost of credit and it has succeeded to drawing low-cost funding from national and international agencies (Jain, 1996). Its performance over the years, however, contradicts the gloomier views reflected in the above criticisms. Without confronting the rural power elite directly, it has expanded credit facilities to 2 million rural families, about one-fifth of the total landless in Bangladesh. Beginning with its conceptual link of poverty, Grameen may be credited as being different to the other organisations in many different aspects:

- Grameen was designed on the proposition that credit is a human right and the poor are entitled to have access to credit in order to improve their lives. It discards the traditional wisdom of the non-bankability of the poor;
- it is not aimed at creating wage-employment, but towards generating self-employment;
- it goes to the borrowers, not the other way round;
- Grameen is manned by energetic and innovative youths, with a thorough understanding of the socio-economic context in which the bank has to operate;
- Grameen officials have no functional relationship with the rural elite, nor does the operational framework allow them to participate as clients or as patrons;
- it has developed a mechanism to bypass the state-controlled institutions;
- it is a bank absolutely for the poor, who share 75% of the bank's ownership;
- the culture of corruption has yet to take its roots in Grameen.

Grameen has been accepted as a replicable model during the 1980s in a number of countries (Hulme, 1990; Gibbons, 1991; Rahman, 1993). Replicability of poverty-focused rural development programmes has to be treated with caution as several successful and acclaimed pilot projects failed to deliver when replicated. The applicability of a Grameen financial system has been examined in several programmes in Malaysia, Barkina Faso, Malawi, Tanzania, Pakistan, Philippines, Sri Lanka, USA and Bangladesh. Indonesia, Vietnam, Mali, Nepal, and Chile have also developed rural programmes based upon the Grameen model. The experience of the partial or total replication of the Grameen model in developing countries suggests that it has an efficient operative mechanism to explore the potential of the landless and poor.

Hulme (1990) developed four propositions regarding the feasibility of replicating Grameen. The first proposition relates to the replication of a Grameen model in its present form on a national scale. The underlying assumptions in this case are:

- both Bangladesh and the host country have a similar socio-economic environment;
- the implementation workers of the host country possess the same expertise and personal qualities as Grameen workers;
- the knowledge and experience of the bank is readily transferable to the institutions of the host country.

The second proposition related to the application of Grameen as an initial model for an action research project, and it assumes that:

- the socio-economic and political environment of Bangladesh and the host country are almost similar and experimentation can cope with the differences;
- organisations can be created and personnel can be located who have or can be trained to have the relevant skill and attitude to run a Grameen-like institution;
- if the experiment proves to be successful than it can be gradually expanded.

The third proposition suggested that Grameen is not directly replicable, but some of its policies and features may be transferred. It recognises that the environmental differences are significant, and the whole package of the institutional structure and culture are not transferable except for some of its relevant policies. The fourth proposition asserts that Grameen is not replicable, and little can be learned from it. This proposition banks on the assumptions that Grameen's uniqueness reflected in a high degree of subsidy, the personality and charisma of its founder, and a specific socio-economic condition. The institutions have to learn their own lessons (*ibid.*). The fourth proposition is espoused by the public sector bankers espouse, whilst the first one has proved to be attractive to some political activists. Fuglesang and Chandler (1986) support the third proposition. Yunus himself promoted the idea to take Grameen as an action research project, and to expand or to wind up subject to the degree of success (Rahman, 1993).

Hulme (1990), Gibbons (1990), and Rahman (1993), who confirmed the success of Grameen, examined several rural financing programmes modelled on it. In most programmes the target group was reached with a rate of loan recovery varying from 75% (Project Nirdhan in Nepal) to 100% (Project Karya Usaha Mandiri in Indonesia). On the transferability of Grameen as a package, Hossain (1988) maintained that it had a fair chance of success in densely settled, poverty stricken areas, though not as a fixed prescription. Grameen itself was derived from an action research project and evolved through several stages, namely experimental (at Zobra in Chittagong), pilot/demonstration (in Chittagong and Tangail) and production or replication (nationwide). The phasing helped Grameen planners and promoters to cope with what Rondinelli (1983) defined as the stages of ignorance, uncertainty, and complexity. Grameen followed a pattern of projects, which are planned:

> incrementally and adaptively by desegregating problems and formulating responses through a process of decision making that joins learning with action (Rondinelli, 1983:89).

Grameen has been viewed as a model of institutional development in raising the accessibility to development for poor people.

Is Grameen an alternative to land reform?

A comprehensive study by Ray (1987) concluded that Grameen had enabled the landless rural poor to come out of poverty without bringing about changes in the property relations. The rural elite continued to hold their tight grip on the poor through their ability to distribute economic and social favour, but in the Grameen villages, the grip has loosened. With their access to money, the poor clients no longer seek their favour. It has succeeded in circumventing some of the traditional sources of the power, controlled and directed by the rural elite. The unique participatory process among the poor clients enables them make their way out of the local power without confronting them.

Except for undertaking the risk of ecological damage by depopulating the declining forest cover, there is no scope for expanding agriculture's horizontal base. Considering the extent of potential claimants for land on the one hand, and the extreme scarcity of supply on the other, it does not appear that distribution of land for cultivation under the existing institutions would be an effective attack on landlessness and rural poverty. The distributive land reform would not produce economically viable parcels and cannot be successfully administered with the existing bureaucratic apparatus in the prevailing socio-economic and political context. This paper emphasises that the distribution of agricultural land under a land reform programme is a relatively weak tool to fight the poverty of the recipient families. Under any ideological regime, Marxist or capitalist, productivity and social justice remain central to the policy logic of land reform (Herring, 1983). The arguments of the inverse relationship of farm size and productivity, and inefficiency of share tenancy, are advanced from the economic premise to undertake redistributive land reform. The technological regime has weakened the small farm size based argument of higher productivity. The landholder's role of trinity 'owner-lender-trader' has shrunk due to the interventionist nature of development institutions and the wider infiltration of the market. It also appears that the decline in the degree of deprivation of tenants has reduced the degree of inefficiency entailed with sharecropping, although insecurity of tenancy still remains high.

Ladejinsky (1970) detected that the heart of the problem for agrarian economy lies in the countryside and the pivot of the national economy is embedded in agriculture. But for Bangladesh, 'the heart of the problem' has remained in the countryside, although 'the pivot of national economy' has started to stage a departure from the agrarian to the non-agrarian sector. This paper does not subscribe to the popular view that a radical redistribution of land would effectively attack rural poverty in Bangladesh. The Bangladesh situation does not permit one to agree with Berry and Cline (1981) that the formation of an increasing number of small farms out of larger farms would significantly increase employment. Agriculture in Bangladesh is already highly labour intensive. Labour-intensive small farms have limited capacity to absorb the existing labour force. Rural industrialisation could be an effective attack on the sluggish growth of the rural economy and unemployment. However, a catalogue of constraints (lack of entrepreneurs, rural credit, market, and infrastructure, centralisation of authority and large and urban enterprises-bias) has impeded the growth of the rural industries. However, the non-farm sector within Grameen's operational model has shown definite promise. The equation of land and landless has suggested that the scope for solving the rural problems with land reform is limited. It has been roughly estimated that Grameen and similar other RFIs have meanwhile integrated about 4 million households into some institutional framework to combat poverty. Based on the success of Grameen type of credit in addressing the rural landless the following policy measures is suggested:

Continue to expand the coverage of Grameen to all other rural villages not covered under or poorly covered by the Non-Government Organisations.

Conclusions

The Grameen experience suggests that in the existing socio-economic and political context of Bangladesh, landless and land-poor can best be served through regulated small credit, not with land. Grameen has received a wide audience, and is being replicated in a number of countries. It is a big shift from the conventional economic theory and practice, envisaging credit as a human right, and proposing that channelling credit, without any collateral, to the poor entails no more risk than advancing credit to the rich with high collateral. The bank relies on the borrowers' potential, their collective responsibility and its own incentive structure. Over a decade of its operation as a bank for the rural poor, it has disproved certain long-held established myths relating to the ability of the poor and capacity of the credit, namely:

- poor people are not bankable;
- credit becomes useless unless it comes in a package with training, technology and marketing;
- poor people use credit for meeting immediate and pressing consumption needs; and
- credit is too weak a tool to restructure the social order.

It has developed a reoriented humanised and flexible bureaucracy, which reaches the doorstep of the poor instead of asking them to come to the banks. Grameen, a rural financial institution, is a success story in creating self-employment and generating income. If the access to land of the landless and land-poor people is conceived as an essential goal of land reform, Grameen has surely initiated an alternative land reform without calling for charitable distribution of land or any other state intervention. In the Grameen way, economic empowerment has brought about changes in the rural households and has probably signalled a change in tenure relations in an iniquitous social structure. Blair (1985:1243) notes that 'between false starts, loss of nerves and abrupt changes of the government', Bangladesh has lost the opportunity to build participatory institutions. Grameen has probably created an environment which has a wider implication in the development of democratic institutions. The question of sustainability of the institution of Grameen may be raised as a second-generation problem. By now it has emerged as a huge organisation. It is yet to show major wounds of institutional rapture. The author, like many other sceptics, would not be surprised to be reported of dysfunction and maladministration in Grameen. Is not it the right time to split the organisation into small and independent functional units? Decentralisation and a loose co-ordination would have been a good idea in coping with risks entailed with large organisations. Studies on Grameen by the new generation of management scholars are essential toward effective and sustainable management of this organisation.

References

Ahluwalia, M.S., 1990. Policies for poverty alleviation, *Asian Development Review*, **8**(1), 111-132.

Alavi, H., 1973, The state in the postcolonial societies: Pakistan and Bangladesh. In: Gough, K. & Sharma, H.P. (eds.), *Imperialism and Revolution in South Asia*, Monthly Review Press, London, 59-81.

Berry, R.A. & Cline, W.R., 1979. *Agrarian Structure and Productivity in Developing Countries*, John Hopkins University Press, Baltimore.

Blair, H.W., 1978. Rural development, class structure and bureaucracy in Bangladesh, *World Development*, **6**(1), 65-82.

Boyce, J.K., 1987. *Agrarian Impasse in Bengal: Agricultural Growth in Bangladesh and West Bengal, 1949-1980*, Oxford University Press, Oxford.

Braverman, A. & Gausch, J., 1986. Rural credit markets and institutions in developing countries: lesson for policy analysis from practice and theory, *World Development*, **14**(10-11), 53-69.

Braverman, A. & Gausch, J., 1993. Administrative failure in government credit programme. In: Hoff, K., Braverman, A. & Stiglitz, J. (eds.), *The Economics of Rural Organisation: Theory, Practice and Policy*, Oxford University Press, Oxford, 53-69.

Bullard, R., 1993. Tenure to hold, *Our Common Estate*, RICS, London.

Elson, D., 1991. Structural adjustment: its effect on women. In: Wallace, T. & March, C. (eds.), *Changing Perceptions: Writings on Gender and Development*, Oxfam Publications, Oxford, 39-53.

Fuglesang, A. & Chandler, D., 1993. *Participation as Process - Process as Growth*, Grameen, Dhakar.

Ghayur, S., 1990. Non-farm employment in rural areas of the SAARK region, *Journal of Rural Development and Administration*, **XXII**(1), 17-37.

Gibbons, D.S., 1991. *Replication of the Grameen Bank Financial System*, Grameen Bank, Dhaka.

Hashemi, S.M., Schuler, S.R. & Riley, A., 1996. Rural credit programs and women's empowerment in Bangladesh, *World Development*, **24**(4), 635-652.

Herring, R.J., 1983. *Land to the Tiller: The Political Economy of Agrarian Reform in South Asia*, Yale University Press, New Haven.

Hoff, K. & Stiglitz, J.E., 1993. Imperfect information and rural credit markets: puzzles and policy perspectives. In: Hoff, K., Braverman, A. & Stiglitz, J.E. (eds.), *The Theory of Rural Organisation: Theory, Practice and Policy, Oxford University Press, Oxford*, 33-52.

Hossain, M., 1984. *Credit for Alleviation of Rural Poverty: The Experience of Grameen Bank in Bangladesh*, Bangladesh Institute of Development Studies, Dhaka.

Hossain, M., 1988. *Credit for Alleviation of Rural Poverty: The Grameen Bank in Bangladesh*, International Food Policy Research Institute, Washington, D.C.

Hossain, M., 1989. *Green Revolution in Bangladesh: Impact on Growth and Distribution of Income*, University Press Limited, Dhaka.

Hulme, D., 1990. Can Grameen Bank be replicated? Recent experiments in Malaysia, Malawi and Sri Lanka, *Development Policy Review*, **8**(3), 287-300.

Jain, P., 1996. Managing credit for the rural poor: Lessons from the Grameen Bank, *World Development*, **24**(1), 79-89.

Khandaker, S., Khalily, B. & Khan, Z., 1994. *Is Grameen Bank Sustainable?* World Bank, Washington D.C.

Lappe, F. & Collins, J., 1977. *Food First: Beyond the Myth of Scarcity*, Houghton Mifflin, Boston.

Momen, M.A., 1996. Land reform and landlessness in Bangladesh. Unpublished PhD Thesis, School of Surveying, University of East London.

Osmani, S.R., 1989. Limits to the alleviation of poverty through non-farm credit, *The Bangladesh Development Studies*, **XVIII**(4), 1-19.

Prosterman, R.L., Temple, M.N. & Hanstad, T.M., 1990. Introduction. In: Prosterman, R.L., Temple, M.N. & Hanstad, T.M. (eds.), *Agrarian Reform and Grassroots Development: Ten Case Studies*, Lynne Rienner Publishers, Boulder, Colorado, 1-11.

Rahman, A., 1993. Rural development from below: lessons learned from Grameen Bank experience in Bangladesh. In: Quddus, M.A. (ed.), *Rural Development in Bangladesh: Strategies and Experiences*, BARD, Comilla.

Rahman, A., Wahid, A.N.M. & Islam, F., 1993. Impact of Grameen Bank on the nutritional status of the rural poor. In: Wahid, A.N.M. (ed.), *The Grameen Bank: Poverty Relief in Bangladesh*, Westview Press, Boulder, Colorado, 76-126.

Ravallion, M., 1989. Land-contingent poverty alleviation schemes, *World Development*, **17**(8), 1223-1233.

Ray, J.K., 1987. *To Chase A Miracle: A Study of Grameen Bank of Bangladesh*, UPL, Dhaka.

Raymer, S., 1975. The nightmare of famine, *National Geographic*, July 1975.

Rondinelli, D.A., 1990. *Development Projects and Policy Experiments: An Adaptive Approach to Development Administration*, Routledge, London.

Safilos-Rothschild, C., 1991. Gender and rural poverty in Asia: implication for agricultural project design and implementation, *Asia-Pacific Journal of Rural Development*, 1(1), 41-61.

Shams, K., 1992. *Devising Effective Credit Delivery System for the Poor: The Grameen Bank Experience*, Grameen Bank, Dhaka.

Siamwalla, A., 1993. Rural credit and rural poverty. In: Quibria, M.G. (ed.), *Rural Poverty in Asia: Priority Issues and Policy Options*, Asian Development Bank, Manila, 287-315.

Stiglitz, J.E., 1993. Peer monitoring and credit markets. In: Hoff, K., Braverman, A. & Stiglitz, J.E. (eds.), *The Economics of Rural Organisation: Theory, Practice and Policy*, World Bank, Washington D.C., 70-86.

Todd, H., 1996. *Women at the Centre: Grameen Bank - Borrowers after One Decade*, University Press Limited, Dhaka.

Wahid, A.N.M. & Rahman, A., 1993. The Grameen Bank and the power of rural administrative elite in Bangladesh. In: Wahid, A.N.M. (ed.), *The Grameen Bank: Poverty Relief in Bangladesh*, Westview Press, Boulder, Colorado, 155-174.

Wood, G.D., 1994. *Bangladesh: Whose Ideas, Whose Interests?* IT Publications, London.

World Bank, 1989. *World Development Report 1989: Financial Systems and Development*, World Bank, Washington D.C.

Yaron, J., 1994. What makes rural finance institutions successful? *The World Bank Research Observer*, 9(1), 49-70.

Yunus, M., 1982. *Grameen Bank Project in Bangladesh - A Poverty Focused Rural Development Programme*, Grameen Bank, Dhaka.

Yunus, M., 1983. *Rural Development: A New Development Strategy, Not A Development Priority*, Grameen Bank, Dhaka.

Yunus, M., 1993. *The Poor as Engine of Development. Grameen Booklet*, Grameen Bank, Dhaka.

Yunus, M., 1994a. *Grameen Bank - Does the Capitalist System Have to be the Handmaiden of the Rich?* Grameen Bank, Dhaka.

Yunus, M., 1994b. *Grameen Bank: Experiences and Reflections*, Grameen Bank, Dhaka.

The cadastral system of Kiev City: managing real estate registration and asset valuation

Mark DEAKIN
School of the Built Environment, Napier University, Edinburgh

Abstract

This paper outlines the attempts made over the past few years to develop the cadastre required by Kiev City Council's property management division to function as a privatisation authority - to develop, that is, what the paper refers to as the financial aspects of the cadastral system: or to be more precise; the real estate registration, asset valuation and leasing services, which the property management division of Kiev City require to participate in the privatisation, economic reform and process of liberalisation Ukraine has become subject to since the break-up of the former USSR. The examination draws upon research recently undertaken as part of a British Know How Fund project investigating the development of financial services for the property management division of Kiev City. It also draws upon data and information provided about the cadastral system in Kiev City by the State Property Fund, Kiev Project Team and Institute of Socio-Economic problems for the City. The fund, team and institute, who along with the property management division of Kiev City, act as the local privatisation authority responsible for the design of the cadastre, registration of real estate and valuation of assets under the emerging structure of tenure.

Introduction

Since the 'rent as tax' debate of *glasnost* and *perestroika*, the development of an efficient cadastral system in Kiev City has become increasingly important. This paper will examine how the cadastre has been re-designed under the *post-communist* era to act as a financial mechanism for the management of real estate registration and valuation of assets subject to some form of lease under the privatisation programme. In this endeavour it will draw attention to the legal basis of the privatisation programme, the financial aspects of the cadastral system, the management of real estate registration and the asset valuation procedures regulating the price property should transfer under the emerging structure of tenure. The paper will suggest that the cadastral system developed for the taxation of land reflects a number of assumptions about the nature of rent which are questionable under the privatisation programme and financial mechanisms (i.e. provisions for the management of real estate registration and asset valuation) it seeks to develop as part of the reforms and liberalisation currently making up Ukraine's transition to a market economy. It will also propose that while the gaps between the old and new are considerable, the confusion surrounding the development of the cadastral system as a financial mechanism for the registration of real estate and valuation of assets, lies in the changing nature of rent under the privatisation programme and transitional strategy adopted to instrumentalise such a payment (not as a tax on land, but as a price reflecting the market value of property).

The cadastre

The legal basis for the cadastre is set out in the *1991 Principles of the USSR and Non-Republic Legislation of Land*. The principles set out in this legislation regulate the use of land and aim to bring about a more rational, economic and efficient use of land[1]. The particular aims and objectives of the State cadastre appear under Articles 48-49 of Section XII. These articles state that the cadastre is intended to provide the 'Soviets of the People's Deputies', enterprises, institutions, and organisations of the former USSR, with information about landed resources, graduated taxes and rental payments. As such, it is required to provide essential data about the legal status of landed assets, the type of assets, i.e. fixed or circulating, and their distribution among enterprises. It is also required to hold information on payments for the employment of goods and services by an enterprise, profit on trade, economic planning zones and the coefficients required for the taxation of land.

As a comprehensive data-base, it covers all enterprises in Kiev City and in this capacity provides:

- a complete register of physical and legal characteristics for development sites and both the fixed and circulating assets of land use establishments;
- the charges paid by enterprises for the supply of goods and services made use of in industry, trade and commerce;
- the profit on enterprise land use establishments generate;
- the economic planning zones Kiev City has compiled to bring about a more rational, economic and efficient use of land;
- the coefficients required for the taxation of land.

Taking the form of a computer-based information system, the database has been designed by the Kiev Project Team. This institute and the division of labour covers research and development, data collection employ about 30 property managers, programme design, information processing and application. The information forming the database is held on a mainframe computer within the institute's headquarters and the team has ultimate authority over the use of that information by the City's property management division.

The rent as tax debate

Article 12 of the 1991 Principles referred to earlier, relates to the matter of land taxation. From studies carried out under the price-liberalisations of glasnost and perestroika, it had been found that industry, trade and commerce treated land as a free gift of nature, unrestricted and plentiful in supply. The surveys undertaken also identified great areas of land, which were left unoccupied and without beneficial use. In an attempt to rationalise the use of land and reflect its limited supply, the State proposed that prices ought be charged for the use of land and such 'rental payments' should be paid to the appropriate City authorities. As a system of taxation affecting the country as a whole, it is proposed that the price charged for the use of land should be calculated on the basis of the following formula:

$$C = CU \times CI \times CS$$

Where: *C* equals the coefficient of zonal profit from an establishment's use of land;

CU is the value of the city in which the enterprise takes place;
CI represents the value of the economic planning zone in which the subject is found; and
CS is the value of the attributes specific to the land use location in this zone of the city.

Using this formula, the property management division of Kiev City carried out a comprehensive assessment of each land use establishment's tax liability between 1991 and 1993.

Table 1 Demographic, land value and infrastructure statistics

Indicators	Measurement Units	Kiev	Zones					
			1	2	3	4	5	6
Territory	Population per hectare	84.8	6.4	2.1	11.9	24.8	10.0	1.0
Population	Total	3,100	534	235	955	1,600	10.0	1.0
Land values	Roubles	28.7	6.9	3.7	7.7	13.3	0.3	0.4
Infrastructure and public service costs	Roubles	25.2	5.4	2.8	6.5	12.7	0.3	0.2

Notes: The territorial and population figures are multiples of 1,000 and the land value, infrastructure and public service costs represents billions of roubles.

Zone 1 is the central zone including the territories on the left and right banks of the River Dnieper. This zone has an abundance of public services and includes the core administrative, commercial and cultural centres.

Zone 2 contains a mixture of retail, office and mass-produced housing estates of the 1950s. This zone is situated in the middle of the city.

Zone 3 comprises the adjacent territories including office and industrial land uses located around and adjacent to Zones 1 and 2.

Zone 4 contains the new housing developments of the 1970s onwards.

Zone 5 consists of residential and industrial estates situated in the city's green belt.

Zone 6 is located in the green belt and is made up of parks and woodland.

The findings of the study are shown in the summary statistics of Table 1, which illustrates the total number of people that are resident in Kiev City, the population densities and land values by economic planning zones. It also shows there are currently six such zones within Kiev requiring a breakdown of *C* by territory and type of sector i.e. primary, secondary and tertiary activities.

Table 2 Coefficients by economic planning zone

Zone	Industry & Construction			Services		
	CU	*CI*	*CU x CI*	*CU*	*CI*	*CU x CI*
Core	3	2.62	7.86	3	5.16	15.48
City centre	3	1.67	5.01	3	3.16	9.48
Adjacent territory	3	0.97	2.91	3	1.52	4.53
Periphery	3	0.91	2.73	3	0.90	2.70
Housing estates in woodland zone	3	0.74	2.13	3	0.93	2.79
Woodland zone	3	0.74	2.13	3	0.43	1.29

The breakdown of coefficient values is not provided in the summary statistics, but these figures are shown in Tables 2 and 3. The summary statistics only serve to show the land values by economic planning zone and not their composition in terms of profit components for *CU, CI* and *CS*. However, putting this aside, they do serve to illustrate the pattern of land values and the fact that the study anticipated the imposition of the tax and payment of rent would generate 28.7 billion roubles (1991 values) of income to the City.

In theory, the zone coefficients measure the potential profit of the land use establishment and the real current cost, it is thought, should be paid in the form of rent. As a form of rent, the zone coefficients have their origins in the 1991 Principles of land taxation. This legislation makes provision for a tax on the use of land through the introduction of a 'graduated system' of rental payments. Under this provision, it is proposed that the calculation of the zone coefficients ought to take place within a national framework and these figures should form the basis of local calculations. It is understood that *CU* has been drawn up in accordance with the coefficients of population sizes and density for cities and measures the average rate of profit on enterprise for Kiev. It is also understood that *CI* represents the coefficient of profit on enterprise by land use establishment in relationship to an economic planning zone. This is a figure worked out on the basis of the ratio between the value of land use establishment in a zone and average rate of profit on the enterprise. *CS* is a coefficient that picks up a rate of profit on enterprise not directly related to population density, in terms of either its territorial or sectoral composition in an economic planning zone, but measures the residual element contingent on a land use establishments' income over cost ratio in location to specific attributes. What is made clear is that rent is seen to represent the difference between the average rate of profit and the specific value of land use establishments i.e. the margin of measurement between *CU*, *CI* and *CS* [2].

Table 3 Coefficients for specific features

Coefficients	Industry & Construction	Services
Most important city thoroughfares	1.05	1.05
Public transport within walking distance	-	1.04
Within walking distance to city centre	-	1.04
Historical centre	1.08	1.88
Restricted building zone	1.06	1.06
Nature conservation area	-	1.07
Environmental protection zone	-	1.06
Recreation grounds	-	1.06

Note: The coefficients measure 1,000 units of Karbovantsi as the post-independence Ukranian currency. It is also understood the coefficients are linked to an inflation index and are to be upwardly adjusted at the end of each financial year. The coefficients represented here are taken from the 1992 *Guidelines on the Valuation of Fixed and Circulating Assets* [3].

It is perhaps in this way that the appropriation of income in the form of rent proposes to normalise profit on enterprise. If this is correct, there appears to be a strong likelihood that many of the land use establishments in the peripheral zones outwards will pay no rent because the rates of profit are below the average. Tables 2 and 3 illustrate the composition of the coefficients in question by each of the six economic planning zones and by both territory and sector. Table 2 shows the composition of *CU* and *CI*.

Table 3 relates to *CS* and illustrates what effect such factors have on the composition of *C*.

At the time of preparing the paper, there were two main issues forming the subject of Presidential Decrees: one on the full deregulation of prices for energy, coal in particular and the adoption of a land tax. At present, there is no evidence to suggest the land tax proposal has been adopted in practice. For now, its significance appears to lie in the fact it provides a possible source of income to fund State budgets and the theoretical basis for the valuation of assets subject to privatisation (Deakin, 1995, 1996, 1997a, 1997b).

Re-designing the cadastre

The paper has so-far drawn attention to the cadastre and the rent as tax debate surrounding the principles of the USSR and non-republic legislation on land. The remainder of the paper will look at how the cadastre has been re-designed under the post-communist era to act as a financial mechanism for the registration of real estate and valuation of assets subject to privatisation. This examination will begin by looking at the privatisation programme the cadastre now serves and go on to examine the financial aspects of the cadastral system.

The privatisation programme

In accordance with the Law on the Ownership of Property, Kiev City has defined the objectives of the authority's privatisation programme as follows:

- the de-monopolisation of the city economy to provide for a more efficient and effective utilisation of resources;
- to allow for the development of a market economy;
- to provide income to fund the State budget.

The objectives indicate that the underlying philosophy of the privatisation programme is utilitarian in nature and seeks to de-monopolise the city economy through the development of markets capable of bringing about an efficient and effective use of resources (European Bank for Reconstruction and Development, 1993). To the extent this also requires a transfer of ownership, it is evident Kiev City proposes that the earnings released from the programme of privatisation should provide income to fund the State budget. To meet these objectives, the City compiles a list of land use establishments and development sites to be privatised. The list of subjects represents the annual programme of properties to be privatised by the authority and includes enterprises from the following sectors of the economy:

- stores, trade centres and markets;
- public catering, canteens, cafeteria, cafes and bars;
- services - repair shops, laundries, dry cleaners, dressmakers, furniture repair and restoration;
- municipal services - hotels;
- all branches of building materials.

The Law on the Privatisation of Small Enterprises refers to trade, food consumption, domestic consumer services, light industry, construction suppliers and some forms of transportation. Under this law it is possible for fixed assets in terms of the plant, machinery and premises of land use establishments to be privatised unless protected by the Local Council of People's Deputies (Fryman, 1993). By contrast, small-scale privatisation in most other former Soviet States only allows for the leasing rather than full transfer of property ownership (Kaser, 1995).

From the list of subjects, it is evident that the privatisation process is focused on the transfer of property ownership in the construction, distribution and retail services of small-scale State enterprises. It appears that Kiev City is of the opinion that such a small-scale construction, distribution and retail privatisation will cause the least amount of disruption to industry and trade and so allow the required economic reforms and liberalisation to go ahead with the minimal amount of structural upheaval. It should be noted that, at the time of preparing this paper, the property management division of Kiev City had no mass privatisation programme. It is only since February 1995 that the Parliament of the Ukraine has given the question of mass privatisation any serious consideration. For the moment, the privatisation programme is seen to be small scale aimed at the construction, distribution and retail sectors (Kaser, 1995).

The financial aspects of the cadastral system

These concern the procedures Kiev City's property management division are required to implement in order for the ownership of a subject to be transferred under the programme of privatisation[4]. In all, it is possible to identify eight procedures the property management division has to take into consideration. Together they form what is referred to here as the financial aspects of the cadastral system under the privatisation programme and include the following:

- the survey of the property forming the subject of privatisation;
- the setting up of funds and accounting units for establishments making up the enterprises in question;
- the registration of the real estate forming the establishment;
- the valuation of development sites, fixed and circulating assets forming the land use;
- the collection of any tax charged on the use of land;
- the formulation of the leasehold agreement governing the use of a landed asset transferred under the process of privatisation;
- the distribution of privatisation proceeds to the appropriate State budgets;
- the management of any retained interest in an establishment.

As has already been pointed out, the above make up the financial aspects of the cadastral system, or what might be more accurately referred to as services the property management division has sought to develop in order for Kiev City to function as a privatisation authority. The paper will examine this development under four headings. In doing so it will ignore the first two services and focus attention on the questions surrounding the registration of real estate, valuation of assets, taxation of land and formulation of leasehold agreements. This will be done under the following titles: real estate registration, asset valuation, rent under the privatisation programme, and lease governing the emerging structure of tenure.

Real estate registration

Figure 1 shows the data that can be accessed on the terminals within the property management division. It shows the nature, type and extent of information held on each land use establishment and provides the basic physical, legal *and* financial information required by the property management division to carry out asset valuations and calculate the 'price-value' of subjects it is proposed should be transferred under the privatisation programme.

At this stage, it is perhaps worthwhile noting that the compilation of the computer-based information system is seen by some commentators as too slow and costly an exercise and one which is having the effect of focusing the authority's mind on real estate registration rather than asset valuation and calculation of price-values. Such commentators see the focus of attention on the former rather than the latter as unfortunate. This is because it has the unfortunate effect of concentrating attention on the practicalities of real estate registration and tends to ignore the more controversial questions surrounding the theory - not to mention the methods and techniques - of asset valuation under the price-value calculations of the privatisation programme.

The degree to which it is possible to establish whether or not there is any substance in such a view depends to a large extent on the subtle, if somewhat critical, distinction drawn between *rent as a tax on land and as a price that reflects the market value (i.e. scarcity and transfer earnings) of property* under the privatisation programme and emerging structure of tenure.

Keeping this question in mind, the following section will look at where rent fits into the price-value formula represented as $V + C = V_z$ and what bearing this has on the valuation of assets. To do this it will be necessary to look at the theoretical basis of the book value (V) and real current cost (C) components of V_z (where V_z is the price-value of the assets under the privatisation programme) and the particular understanding of the capital-income relationship it draws on to transform profit into rent and both into a form of tax on the use of land. Having already set out the basis of rent as a form of tax, the paper will proceed by examining the formula for the valuation of assets and some of the difficulties it experiences in attempting to transform the fiscal representation of rent as a land tax into a mechanism for the calculation of prices reflecting the market-value of property transferred under the privatisation programme.

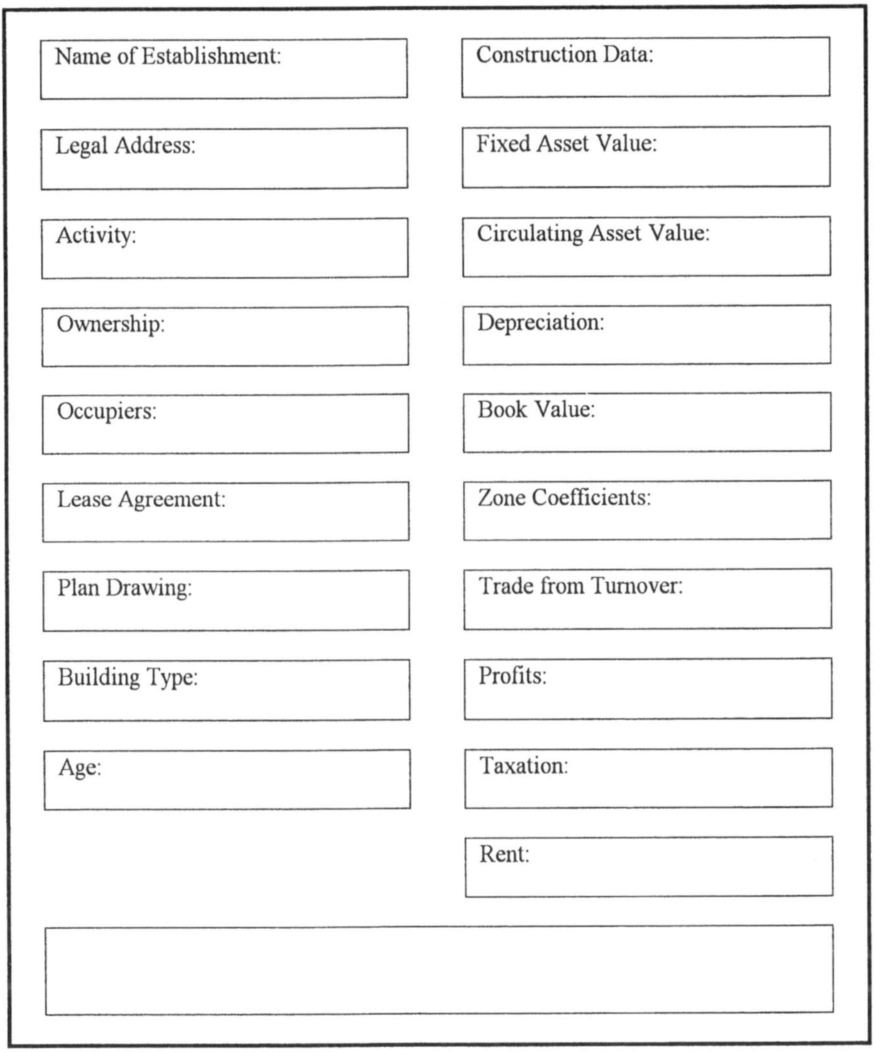

Name of Establishment:	Construction Data:
Legal Address:	Fixed Asset Value:
Activity:	Circulating Asset Value:
Ownership:	Depreciation:
Occupiers:	Book Value:
Lease Agreement:	Zone Coefficients:
Plan Drawing:	Trade from Turnover:
Building Type:	Profits:
Age:	Taxation:
	Rent:

Figure 1 Data accessible from the Property Management Division

Put in slightly different terms, the difficulties and problems this representation of rent as either a fiscal or market phenomenon poses not only for the property management division of Kiev City in the valuation of assets and calculation of price-values under the privatisation programme, but for the development of the markets on which the whole process of economic reform and liberalisation in Ukraine depends. While such a representation of the difficulties and problems may appear a little dramatic, it nonetheless goes someway to illustrate the critical role that property management plays in the logic of economic reform and liberalisation under the transition. It is felt worthwhile making this point at a relatively early stage in the paper because questions of asset valuation and transfer price calculation tend to be overlooked in the literature that currently exists on matters surrounding the transition.

Asset valuation

Under the privatisation programme the properties forming the subject of transfer are referred to as independent enterprises but known as land use establishments. In the majority of cases, the privatisation programme requires that the transfer of such land use establishments take place via auction and this goes ahead on the basis of book value, plus the real current cost of assets. Under this scheme the valuation of assets and calculation of price-values proceeds on the basis of the following formula:

$$V_z = V + C$$

Where:

V_z is the price-value of the assets taking into account the zone coefficients;
V is the initial price-value of the fixed and circulating assets of land use establishments; and
C is the coefficient reflecting the potential profitability of a land use establishment within the economic planning zones of Kiev City.

Under this formula, V represents the book value of fixed and circulating assets forming the land use establishments. As to what is referred to as the initial price-value, it represents the historic cost of the assets, written down by the amount of depreciation they have been subject to. Here, depreciation represents the process of amortisation and as an accounting concept is linked to debt repayment and is not related to either the physical or economic life of

38

the subjects. C is a coefficient made use of to measure the amount of potential profit which the fixed and circulating assets forming the land use establishment are likely to generate from the transfer of ownership and the figure which it is proposed should be added to V in order for the initial price-value to take the coefficient of the relevant economic planning zone into account: for V_z that is, to be the sum of the book value and real current cost, which the formula proposes should form the transfer price under the privatisation programme. While the idea of V representing the book value, as depreciated-historic cost, is not difficult to grasp, the concept of C as the real current cost of assets (and as a coefficient representing the potential profit of an economic planning zone) is a little more difficult to understand and is an issue the paper will examine under the question of rent.

With the fixed and circulating assets of land use establishments, it is the full V_z formula that is made use of as a form of asset valuation. Where a privatisation involves a foreign investor, the V_z formula is modified to take into account of the so-called special coefficients. Here the formula to be used in the calculation of the price-value is:

$$V_z = V + SC$$

where:

V_z is as previously stated;
V initial price-value for the land use establishment or the development site; and
SC is the special coefficient.

At present, no information is available on the composition of the SC components for the V_z formula involving foreign investor participation. All that is known is that such a valuation is carried out in hard currency (usually US dollars, or German Deutschmarks) and provides one of the main opportunities for privatisation authorities to obtain incomes which retain, or increase in value and are capable of being exchanged in the international money markets.

Rent under the privatisation programme

The mass appraisal technique, which the formula provides is unique in that it allows the expert to read off the initial price-values and coefficients and, as a consequence provides a relatively simple solution to the calculation of the price-values required under the provisions of the privatisation programme. While attractive in terms of providing a comprehensive valuation of assets and calculation of price-values, it should be recognised that the mass appraisal technique provides a somewhat novel representation of the income-capital relationship: one that tends to turn the standard income-based logic of Western asset valuation upside down by adding capital and income in the form of the depreciated historic cost, plus potential zonal profit, rather than calculating transfer prices on the basis of net current replacement cost and all that this entails in terms of the cost, capital and income relations more common in market economies.

In many respects, it provides a particular version of the classic problem which surfaces in the valuation of assets and calculation of prices where there is insufficient evidence to pass the market test. In this case, it is the problem of asset valuation and transfer pricing where no formal property markets exist. In market economies, such a problem tends to be confined to the valuation of assets and calculation of transfer prices for what are termed specialist properties - be they under State ownership and held by the public, or private sector[5]. Under economic reform, liberalisation and the logic of transition, it is a problem that relates to the valuation of assets and calculation of prices which fall under the legislative provisions of the privatisation programme and proposals it sets out for the development of property markets; in short, the vast majority of both specialist and non-specialist, or standard property holdings.

It is perhaps for this reason, i.e. the fact it affects the vast majority of property holdings, irrespective of whether it is held under State ownership and made use of in public sector as either a specialist or standard property that the problem appears more acute and difficult to reconcile. In a nutshell, it is the problem of adopting a form of asset valuation and price calculation that reflects not historic, but real, current costs and bases the latter on a transfer figure, which represents the market-value of the property in question. In adopting this Anglo-centric view, it is possible to appreciate the nature and extent of the problem and question whether the line of reason flowing from profits to rent as a tax and on to rent not as a tax but as an independent relation, provides the required form of asset valuation and price calculation. Looked at from the conventions of asset valuation and calculation of transfer prices in the UK, Europe and USA, it no doubt appears a roundabout way of approaching the issue. But, apart from the radical step of transferring property at book value (with a possible clawback based on future prices), there appears to be no other way of grounding the cost, capital and income relations transitional economies face in anything other than profit and the potential it has to be *transformed into rent not as tax but an independent form of income* under the provisions of the privatisation programme.

It is perhaps in this manner that the valuation of assets and calculation of price-values does away with the old and attempts to usher in the new, i.e. the manner in which it does away with the book value of V, or initial price-values of the depreciated historic cost, and ushers in the new in terms of C, the real current cost representing the potential profitability of land use establishments in the economic planning zones. This is illustrated in *the $V + C = V_z$* formula referred to here and the attempt it makes to introduce the idea of current replacement cost in terms of depreciated historic cost, plus potential zonal profit - albeit a form of asset valuation and price-value calculation that as yet fails to meet the market test to which the economic reforms, process of liberalisation and transition aspire.

The lease

Given that the transfer of legal interest is always subject to some form of lease it should be seen as the principal document regulating the ownership and use of property under the emerging structure of tenure.

At present, there are three forms of lease-hold agreement:

- an agreement to regulate the use of land where the employers agree to acquire the fixed and circulating assets, but not the establishment's premises;
- a leasehold agreement for enterprises whose employees agree to acquire both the assets and premises;
- an agreement whereby the enterprise leases all assets.

While significant in terms of the property rights such leases transfer to the possessor, there is little evidence to suggest the form of agreement recognises the subtle, but critical, distinction between occupation, building and ground leases. In view of this, what follows will focus on the main clauses of the leases common to all forms of agreement.

The agreement clause sets out the assets covered by the lease and to whom rent is payable. The clause relating to obligations sets out that the tenant is responsible for maintenance and repairs, and for operating the land use establishment in accordance with any local and national statutes. Here the tenant is also responsible for maintenance and renewal of plant and equipment, and must meet public utility costs. Lastly, the rent is reviewable annually, and the tenant is required to provide documentation to the landlord - presumably in relation to profits and trading accounts - by 20 January of each year. The rights clause sets out the landlord's entitlement to inspect the subject premises and to collect rent, and the tenant's right to trade from the subject premises in terms of the permitted use. A clause on special conditions states that the tenant must carry out refurbishment by a specified date, and that, while the works are carried out, the rent is set at a specified (and presumably reduced) level. A general clause states that the tenant may not abandon the premises without penalty, and late payment of rent attracts a 1% per day penalty. Schedules are also attached to the agreement setting out estimated property values (transfer price), an inventory of assets and breakdown of figures for land/buildings, plant and machinery, and circulating assets. Within the lease, there is also a set of guidelines on rent calculation and payment procedures. The rent rate is dependent on the amount of profits the leaseholder makes running the land use establishment.

The actual rent paid is expressed as a percentage of fixed and circulating asset values. It is proposed that the rent should be revised every month in accordance with the inflation index provided by the Ministry of Finance. The calculation of both the rent rate and rent payable is given by the formula:

$$RR = (PR - T)/(IMFAV + MAV) \times 0.3 \times 100$$

$$AR = RR/1.4 + RR/0.8$$

where:

AR is the actual rate;

RR is the rental rate;

PR are the profits for the calendar year preceeding the rental date(s);

T is the total income tax;

IMFAV are the immovable fixed asset values;

MAV are the movable asset values;

0.3 is the ratio of rent in relation to profits;

1.4 is the differential coefficient for *IMFAV*;

0.8 is the differential coefficient for *MAV*.

From the formula, it is apparent that the net profit figure divided by the value of assets gives the productivity of capital employed in the land use establishment and 30 per cent of this figure is taken to represent rent. This figure is then transformed into an actual rental payment through the application of the coefficients. The exact reason why these particular coefficients are used is not known[6]. But, having said this, the use of the coefficients goes some way to illustrate the distinction between the value of fixed and circulating capital which is normally recognised under the valuation of assets and calculation of price-values. From the formula provided, it appears as though there is a relative shortage of fixtures and these command higher rent than circulating assets.

The relationship between the valuation of assets, calculation of price-values and payment of rent under the leasehold provision of the privatisation programme raises a number of questions. Firstly: why, if the $V + C$ formula is put forward to represent the current replacement cost, does the valuation of assets and calculation of the price-values for the transfer of property become subject to rent under the lease? Secondly, if the lease is subject to rent because it is recognised the depreciated historic cost, plus potential profit does not add up to the current replacement cost, what does it represent? Both questions are important for without the advantage of clarifying exactly what V_z equals, it is difficult to establish whether the valuation of assets and calculation of price-values under the privatisation programme is charging either too much or little for the transfer of property. This is because in the first instance the formula may be seen to double-count the rental component owing to its existence in both V_z and the subsequent rental payments of the lease. In this instance it might be said to over-value and inflate the price of property subject to transfer under the privatisation programme. If V_z is not seen to add up to the current replacement cost (because for some unknown reason it is not possible to assess or calculate it under the formula) the rental payments might be seen as a means to safeguard against any such possible shortfall being lost due to the fact the depreciated historic cost, plus potential zonal profit basis of asset valuation and price calculation may undervalue and deflate the price of property.

At present the lack of data available on the valuation of assets and calculation of price-values makes it impossible to establish exactly what V_z represents, whether it is leading to either an under or over-valuation of assets and what effect this has on the pricing of property[7]. As a consequence, the full significance of the asset valuation and price calculations currently in place is not known. But given both form critical components of the transfers planned under the privatisation programme, the important role they play in the economic reforms and liberalisation should not be underestimated. Given that the programme of privatisation also seeks to establish valuations as a proxy for prices, it is perhaps fair to suggest that in forming a part of the reforms and liberalisation which are currently taking place, assessments and calculations of this kind play a key role in the transition to the perceived efficiencies of a more market-based economy.

The transitional strategy

From this brief examination of the developments associated with the cadastral system, real estate register, valuation of assets and leasing procedures, it is evident that many of the initiatives have their origins in the first round of economic reforms which took place in the price liberalisation of the mid to late 1980s. In terms of the cadastre, it is evident that it has been designed to provide information on landed resources and data required for development of rental payments in the form of a graduated system of taxation. Today the status of the graduated taxation system is unclear in many ways it appears to do little more than provide a framework for the registration of real estate and a theoretical basis for the valuation of assets. This is because *under the privatisation programme the cadastral system has been redesigned to form a financial mechanism for the registration of real estate and valuation of assets* and as such acts as an instrument to transfer the ownership and use of property from the State to the private sector, so dividing the legal status of both into what is in effect a landlord and tenant type relationship. That is, to separate rent from tax and develop the former as a relationship which is independent of the latter.

This is evident in the case of the lease where, unlike the previous situation in which profits transform into rent and the latter manifests itself in the form of a tax, it appears under this arrangement as a payment from the tenant to the landlord providing a transfer earning from what is in effect an income-producing property. But what is noticeable here is that the income stream flows from the profit generated by the independent enterprise as a land use establishment and not the capital employed or tied up in it. Even here though there appears to be no formal, let alone real, connection between the rent from income producing property and the value of fixed capital, or circulating assets it makes use of. In view of this, it might be said that while in such circumstances rent exists as a relationship independent of tax, it fails to have a direct connection with the value of capital for the simple reason there is as yet no such market for the transfer of property. No direct relation - it is important to note - between the rental and capital value of property that might under normal circumstances, i.e. in market economies, represent the price property should transfer owing to the technical possibility which exists for rental income to form the basis of capital value in the subjection of the former to a process of capitalisation. It appears that, unlike the income-based approach to property valuation common in market economies, the real estate registration, asset valuation and calculation of price-values under the given formula needs to be grounded in the notion of profit: in other words the profit rather than rental form of the income-capital relationship. The reason for this is simple: it is because as yet the market for the transfer of property under the privatisation programme is rooted in the idea of profit on enterprise and its worth as an asset capable of meeting the land use establishment's occupational needs. At the moment it appears to be the enterprise needs of land use establishments that forms the centre of attention.

Whether this type of income-producing property will develop rent into what the market yields as a return on the investment of capital and as a rate of interest remains to be seen. Whether or not the formula makes it possible to ground the valuation of assets and calculation of price-values in rent as an independent form of the income-capital relationship is questionable. The idea of rent, not as a novel type of the income-capital relationship, but instead as the basis of transforming profit into first tax and then rental income as an independent form of transfer payment in direct relation to capital, does not appear to have been given much consideration under the legislative provisions of the privatisation programme. Indeed, it appears to represent a complete oversight as there is no evidence of provisions being made in the economic reforms or liberalisation to integrate profit, tax or rental income into the structure of capital markets emerging under the transition. This has to be seen as a serious oversight, for in having given rent the potential to form an independent and direct relationship to capital, the income that it produces is not seen to represent the cost which has to be met for property to become interest-bearing capital in the emerging markets and yield a particular rate of return on investment from transactions taking place under the asset valuation and price-value calculations of the privatisation programme.

In being restricted in this way, rent appears to take on a spatial configuration that has the effect of limiting the possibility of basing asset valuation and price calculations on the discounting of future income by the rate of return interest-bearing capital yields in the process of arriving back at the present value which under normal circumstances property should transfer. While capable of representing rent as a spatial configuration of income, it appears that the formula is unable to recognise the temporal dimension to such payments, or the fact that in taking the form of income on interest-bearing capital it also provides the basis to discount future rental income in arriving back at the present value of property[8]. Or put in slightly different terms: it seems unable to develop a form of rental income that transcends past book values, depreciated historic costs and the real current costs of future potential profits in favour of a formula, method of asset valuation and technique of price calculation which make it possible to discount both the spatial and temporal configuration of rental income in arriving back at the present-value of property under the notion of current replacement cost. Perhaps the pertinant question to ask at this stage is whether the development of markets that permit such a form of income-capital relationship are possible under the formula which exists for the valuation of assets and calculation of price-values?

Conclusions

This paper has looked at the development of the cadastral system in Kiev City and has sought to show how the cadastre has been re-designed under the post-communist era to act as a financial mechanism for the management

46

of real estate registration and valuation of assets subject to some form of lease under the privatisation programme. In doing so it has drawn attention to the cadastral system set up under glasnost and perestroika for the taxation of land and introduction of rental payments to bring about a more rational, economic and efficient use of land. It has also demonstrated how the cadastre put in place to tax land and charge rent, forms the framework and theoretical basis to instrumentalise such payments not as a tax on land, but as a price reflecting the market value of property under the privatisation programme.

It has argued that the gap between the 'old and the new' and confusion surrounding the development of the cadastral system as a financial mechanism, can be traced to the changing concept of rent and the instruments i.e. the management of real estate registration and valuation of assets, adopted as the strategy to transform the payment in question from a tax into a price reflecting the market value of property subject to transfer under the privatisation programme. The paper has suggested that the changing concept of rent is one best described by a shift from a tax on land to the price representing the market value of property. While subtle, it is suggested the distinction is an important one to bear in mind, because it goes some way to explain why the redesigning of the cadastre and its development as a financial mechanism takes the form it does.

For in taking, as it does, a form which is not restricted to the rational management of landed resources, it incorporates a great deal more: a form; that is, which does not limit the rationale of land management to the administration of a tax, but one that instrumentalises rent as a means to demonopolise the city, provide a more economic and efficient use of resources (through the de-statisation and decentering of ownership) and which (via the management of real estate registration, valuation of assets and calculation of prices) helps develop the markets required to transfer property under the reforms and liberalisation of the privatisation programme. This is because under the former, it is only the C of the profit-based land tax that is required to form a rental payment, whereas under the latter it is the V of the real estate registered as forming the fixed and circulating assets of a land use establishment which forms the subject of valuation under the $V + C$ formula and subsequent calculation of V_z as the price property should transfer under the privatisation programme. Here and unlike the former situation, rent does not take the form of a profit-based land tax, but a price taken to reflect the market value of the income payment made *in relation to* the capital tied up in the real estate registered as the fixed and circulating assets of a land use establishment.

In the former it is only land that surfaces under the rent as tax debate surrounding the fiscal requirements of land taxation, with the latter it is *land and capital* which enters into the equation through first of all: the registration of the real estate forming the fixed and circulating assets of a land use establishment and by then subsequently subjecting *this particular* combination of resources to a valuation. To a form of asset valuation that in the first instance, calculates the price reflecting the market value of the subjects in question and which then goes on to adopt this figure as the basis for the income payment required to transfer property through the leasehold structure of tenure emerging under the privatisation programme. While this falls some way short of integrating profit, tax, or rental income into the structure of capital markets developing under the economic reforms and liberalisation of the privatisation programme, it nonetheless marks a significant step forward.

References

Alonso, W., 1967. A reformulation of classical location theory and its relation to rent theory, *Papers of the Regional Science Association*, **19**, 23-44.

Alonso, W., 1972. A theory of the urban land market. In: Stewart, M. (ed.). *The City*, Penguin, London, 107-116.

Antwi, A. & Deakin, M., 1996. Discounting, obsolescence, depreciation and their effects on the environment of cities, *Journal of Financial Management for Property and Construction*, **15**(4), 19-30.

Avis, M., Gibson, V. & Watts, J., 1989. *Managing Operational Property*, University of Reading, Reading.

Baum, A. & Crosby, N., 1995. *Property Investment Appraisal*, Routledge, London.

Baum, A. & Mackmin, D., 1989. *The Income Approach to Property Valuation*, Routledge, London.

Britton, W., Connellan, O. & Crofts, M., 1989. *The Economic, Efficient and Effective Management of Public Sector Landed Estates*, Surrey County Council/Kingston Polytechnic, Surrey.

Britton, W., Connellan, O. & Crofts M., 1991. *The Cost Approach to Valuation*, Kingston Polytechnic, Kingston.

Brown, G., 1991. *Property Investment and the Capital Markets,* Chapman and Hall, London.

Champness, P., 1992. Asset valuation in Europe, *The Journal of Property Valuation and Investment,* **10**(4), 427-437.

Current Digest of the Soviet Press, 1990. *Principles of USSR and Union-Republic Legislation on Land,* **42**(3), 22-26, 36.

Deakin, M., 1995. The development of financial services for the property management division of Kiev City, Ukraine, *Our Common Estate,* RICS, London.

Deakin, M., 1996. The property management division of Kiev City, *Property Management,* **14**(4), 15-26.

Deakin, M., 1997a. The financial aspects of property management: the case of Kiev City, *Journal of Property Finance,* **8**(1), 52-82.

Deakin, M., 1997b. The development of local authority property management 1: the underlying issues, *Journal of Financial Management for Property and Construction,* **2**(2).

Deakin, M., 1997c. The development of local authority property management 2: the application, *Journal of Financial Management for Property and Construction,* **2**(3).

Deakin, M., 1997d. An economic evaluation and appraisal of the effects land use, building obsolescence and depreciation have on the built environment. In: Brandon, P., Lombardi, P. & Bentivenga, V. (eds.), *Evaluation of Buildings for Sustainability,* Chapman and Hall, London, 234-262.

Deakin, M., 1997e. The development of a cadastral system: Kiev City since the rent as tax debate, *Journal of Property Taxation and Assessment,* **2**(3).

European Bank for Reconstruction and Development, 1993. *Economic Review: Annual Economic Outlook,* London.

European Centre for Macroeconomic Analysis of Ukraine, 1996. *Ukranian Economic Trends* (Quarterly update, April, 1996), Ministry of Economy, Kiev.

Fisher, I., 1930. *The Theory of Interest,* August, Kelley M, New York.

Fryman, R., 1993. *The Privatisation Process in Russia, Ukraine and the Baltic States,* Central Europe University Press, Budapest.

Kaser, M., 1995. *Privatisation in the CIS,* Royal Institute of International Affairs, London.

Mills, E., 1967. An aggregate model of resource allocation in a metropolitan area, *American Economic Review,* 7, 197-218.

Mills, E., 1969. The value of urban land. In: Perloff, H. (ed.), *The Quality of the Urban Environment,* John Hopkins Press, Baltimore.

Nove, A., 1988. *The Soviet Economic System,* Unwin Hyman, London.

State Property Fund, 1992. *Guidelines on the Valuation of Fixed and Circulating Assets*, State Administration, Kiev.

Endnotes

[1] The background to the cadastre is documented in Nove (1988). The 1991 Principles are discussed in the Current Digest of Soviet Press (1990).

[2] All matters concerning asset valuation and the calculation of price-values are set out in the State Property Fund's (1992). The demographic and land value issues draw on the publications of Alonso (1967 and 1972) and Mills (1967 and 1969). They are supplemented by original research carried out by Urban Institutes throughout the former USSR during the mid-1980's. However, it has to be recognised the similarity between Alonso and Mills' models are purely formal as the profitability index of the formula is based on average rather than marginal costs or revenues. It should be noted that their model also assumes fully developed, if not perfectly competitive market economies. What is also clear is that while Alonso and Mills draw upon the formal logic of exchange in the theorisation of rent, the coefficients are more empiricist in the sense they are grounded in the logic of a multiple regression analysis relating profit, rent and tax to population density, location of industry and so-called special features of the surrounding environment. This is not, it has to be said, related to either the employment of labour or capital in the enterprise a land use establishment is engaged in.

[3] It is understood these figures represent the coefficients for the average land-use establishments, and any enterprises holding assets above the norm - be they fixed, circulating land or buildings will be charged an extra amount of rent in the form of tax. Given the high degree of standardisation in land use structures, such adjustments for plot size are not normally necessary. However, technically it is possible for the authorities in question to link profits, rent and in this instance tax, to a rate per square metre of site coverage or building floor space.

[4] While the main concern of Kiev City's property management division focuses on the question of privatisation, many of the issues regarding the cadastre, registration of real estate, valuation of assets and so forth, reflect a number of general concerns in the UK, USA and Europe over the management of public sector landed estates as assets. See, for example, Britton *et al* (1989), Avis *et al* (1989). Deakin (1997b; 1997c) also looks at many of the issues surrounding the development of local authority property management.

[5] Baum and Mackmin (1989) discuss this point in their introduction, but they of course limit their examination of valuation to standard properties under the income approach. Britton *et al* (1991) examine the cost approach for specialist

property in the public sector of market economies. Irrespective of whether the valuations are of income, or non income-producing property it has to be remembered that both forms of valuation operate within a fully developed property market and as a consequence represent approaches to property valuation not immediately transferable to economies undergoing economic reform and liberalisation. Champness (1992) also examines some of the issues.

[6] Kaser (1995) suggests the coefficient is made use of because the assessment of values and calculation of prices relate to the date in 1992 when the legislation on privatisation came into force. He proposes that under this formula, asset valuations are updated using an inflation index and the current prices are calculated on the basis of such an index. It is also suggested that in many instances these price calculations are notional in the sense they provide the basis upon which to calculate the rental income paid for the lease of property rather than the capital value of an outright transfer. Presumably having the value of the assets in terms of notional capital transfer prices, it is possible to calculate the appropriate rental charges relative to what form of lease any transfer is subject to i.e. whether it is the form shown in either (1), (2) or (3) outlined here.

[7] Information available from the European Centre for Macroeconomic Analysis of Ukraine (1996) indicates that the confusion over what V_z actually represents and what effects it has on the pricing of property, results from the failure of auctions as a privatisation mechanism and reliance on notional capital transfer price-values for buy-outs and leasing arrangements. The centre in question estimate 80% of small-scale privatisations took place on such a basis. As there was no mass privatisation programme in place until February, 1995 these represent the main forms of privatisation and a situation where there is no transfer of capital as income payments under both these mechanisms take the form of rent. If this is correct then it suggests the possible problem of double-counting the capital and rental component has been avoided.

[8] This is the Fisher (1930) thesis on the valuation of property and that dominates contemporary property valuation as set out in the income approach of Baum & Mackmin (1989), Brown (1991) and Baum & Crosby (1995). For a discussion of the thesis see Antwi and Deakin (1996) and Deakin (1997d).

Going beyond shibboleths: the place of land tenure in urban management in Kenya

Dr. Crispus KIAMBA

Associate Professor, Department of Land Development, and Principal, College of Architecture and Engineering, University of Nairobi

Abstract

The availability of land (for commercial and industrial use, for housing - especially for those who live in poverty and the disadvantaged, infrastructure, public services and the various forms of public space) at reasonable cost, in reasonable amounts, at the proper time, remains one of the most complex tasks of governments in the rapidly urbanising and developing world. In spite of enormous efforts and investment by governments and other bodies, it has been most difficult to find solutions that keep face with the problem. Land prices are rapidly becoming too high for effective government and private sector, land development strategies. The private market for land is also becoming increasingly integrated and accessible only to the rich and upper classes of most societies. Because of increases in land prices and consolidation of most land into the hands of few and rich owners, the hope of ownership of land by the larger proportion of the community is becoming increasingly remote.

Introduction

The problem of the availability of land has persisted despite the paradox that seems inherent in the heart of the question of land tenure. Land is essential to all human activities, limited in quantity, immobile, and permanent, and its value, especially urban land, is heavily dependent on socially created demand and publicly provided services. By its very nature, urban land is a public good with a compelling case for public intervention. The aim of society is to find a system of land tenure that will best optimise the contrary pulls of efficiency or productivity and equity or social justice. Doebele's observations are apt:

Land tenure, therefore, is never an 'either-or' situation. It is, at every historical moment, for every society, a question of striking a balance between the need for social control and fairness in access to land, and an equally pressing need for private initiatives to ensure efficiency, and the satisfaction of the human yearning for territorial association...The task of every nation, therefore is to continually to re-define tenure relationships as between public and private rights (1987:8).

Many nations in the developing world have begun to show concern to appropriate land tenure, its controls, cost and availability. For example, the urgent concern for providing land (and related tenurial issues) for the poor and other disadvantaged groups in urban areas has induced changes of profound significance. Evolving issues of 'the right to land' and 'the right to housing' are clearly too enormous for conventional solutions. Rigidity in tenurial matters, and standards and guidelines for land development, for example, have been modified in the process of adopting new, viable and, hence, realistic approaches. The need for new paradigms and solutions to the land question has never been more urgent. Conventional wisdom and paradigms are no longer tenable. Going beyond shibboleths, conventional wisdom and paradigms, in order to devise new or at least innovative and tenable solutions for the new economic and social realities is imperative.

It is the purpose of this article to outline the place of land tenure in the urban development and management in Kenya. New or at least innovative approaches that have increasingly responded sensitively to the new economic and social realities are presented.

Basis for a land policy

The primary aim of a land tenure policy is to define clearly the measures necessary for achieving optimal land use. Although the most optimal land use should the most economically productive use of land, it should also be sensitive to other less tangible but important aspects of land, e.g., socio-cultural aspects of the society in question. Measures indented to ensure that the available land resources in the country are utilised in the most productive way must therefore be in place. In Kenya for example, the *Sessional Paper No. 1 of 1986 on Economic Management for Renewed Growth*, which set out the basis of development in Kenya in the 1990s and beyond, has put the case succinctly:

Anything short of optimal land use would jeopardise the economic future of the country (GOK, 1986).

In order for any state to be able to justify or explain its strategies for land tenure policy it must sort out what the purpose of its land policy is. It must have some essential national interests in land, or some sort of national view on land relations, which would justify national intervention into land relations in the form of a land policy and related formal, and informal, instruments and/or institutions of land management. In this connection, the following are normally suggested as the components of a national interest in land: effectiveness and efficiency; equity; certainty; safeguarding the state and national patrimony; and recognising the legitimacy of the difference. Efficiency and equity may be seen as economic and social aspects of land policy. Certainty deals more with the administrative and legal aspects. The last two are concerned more with political aspects. These components of land policy are closely linked to each other and, together, they provide a sound rationale for the involvement of the institutions of government in land relations; they provide the principles by which to judge any formulation of national land tenure policy.

The systems of land tenure

Access and management

McLaughlin (1981) defines land tenure as the:

> rights, responsibilities and restraints that individuals and groups have with respect to land.

Under this triad concept, land tenure, therefore, refers to the conditions under which access to land is obtained and its use managed and controlled as a resource. It is therefore the mode of owning or holding rights in land, which embodies legal, formal and other informal arrangements under which people gain access to land and utilise it. The system of land tenure therefore provides the basis against which development and productivity is undertaken by individuals and communities. In Kenya, one or other or combinations of traditional or communal, individual or public tenure govern land. It is important to understand these types (including the relationship between them) in order to determine the place of land tenure, land development and management.

Traditional or communal tenure

Communal tenure involves the occupation and control of land by communities or groups for use by individual members of the group. Under this regime there is usually a recognisable authority or head who controls the process of distribution to those entitled to it. This system that operates in the areas where Kenya's land reform programme in the form of land adjudication and registration and the individualisation of land tenure, has not either been started or completed. Such land is referred to as 'trust land' and the tenure as 'customary' or 'traditional'. Such land, managed under the 'Trust Land Act' of the Laws of Kenya, being unadjudicated and unregistered in individuals, is held by the various local authorises (specifically County Councils) in trust of and for the benefit of the local residents. It is in this communal land tenure regime that the first circuit of land relations is prevalent.

Communal tenure represents a complex network of social, cultural and technical imperatives. When any of these change, the incidents of that tenure regime will also change. This has indeed happened in many parts in Kenya especially under conditions of urbanisation, population pressure and agricultural intensification.

It has long been appreciated that communal land tenure arrangements have important attributes. In some cases the procedure for allocation for use, being vested as it is in a recognisable authority, results in equitable distribution. Where there is instability as a result of disputes arising from lack of clarity in the definition of land rights, these can be resolved through special statutory protection involving, for example, co-operative or corporate registration of groups or group rights along recognisable traditional divisions or units or social organisations. Examples in Kenya include 'group' ownership of land under both the 'Land (Group Representatives) Act' and 'Registered Land Act' of the laws of Kenya, 'community land trust' and 'sectional properties' under the *Sectional Properties Act*. Communal tenure arrangements have, however, been criticised, *inter alia*, for their lack of juridical specificity and apparent insecurity as a vehicle for capital generation in for urban and agricultural development. Largely for this reason, lending institutions and agencies have kept out of the financing of development in areas governed by this type of land tenure.

Individual tenure

Individual tenure, or private landed property, involves registered ownership and, in theory, absolute freedom of use and transfer of rights over a clearly demarcated parcel of land. In many urban areas and smallholder agricultural areas, however, the operation of individual tenure is, in practice, still subject to strong social and cultural forces representing the resilience of communal tenure principles - hence the complex mixture, in practice, of communal and individual land relations as seen later.

The government of Kenya has accepted that the long-term goal of land ownership is to convert the whole or at least a substantial portion of the country to individualised tenure regime. Where this had not been done by the time of independence, 1963, and largely in the areas outside the 'White Highlands' or 'Scheduled Areas', it is being done through the processes of adjudication, consolidation (where appropriate) and the registration of land in accordance with the 'Registered Land Act'. Although the process has now been in operation over three decades, completion of the exercise is no where in sight. The constraints to a speedy process of the individualisation of land tenure include litigation, political interference, finance and administrative problems.

The regime of individual tenure is, therefore, on the face, a creation of the English law and practice received into Kenya by virtue of colonialism. On the whole, individual tenure has been extolled for the security, which it is believed to confer through the grant of indefeasible title (Okoth-Ogendo, 1991). On a deeper level, however, the introduction and evolution of private landed property in Kenya has been a part of the larger process of colonisation, and introduction and maintenance of the predominantly capitalist mode of production in Kenya (Kiamba, 1989). Along with this came the dissolution of the old or customary land relations of the Africans, or at least their transformation to a form compatible with capitalist development. The social basis of the introduction of individual or private landed property relates to several points:

- firstly, the privatisation of land ownership (since land is a condition and an element of production) leads to the opening up of the possibilities for treating it as a commodity, for selling and buying, hence the basis of private accumulation;
- secondly, as one of the requisite conditions of the capitalist mode of production is the capital-labour relation (the formal subjugation of labour by capital), if the full domination of labour by capital is to be achieved, the argument is that a wage labour force, a landless proletariat, is a fundamental condition;
- thirdly, the legal or juridical standing and legitimacy of the

'personification' of land, the most essential condition of production, in a capitalist society has a basis on the 'sanctity' and 'inviolability' of private property (Kiamba, 1989; Harvey, 1982).

Because of their relative insulation from external controls, landholders under private title are prone to the using of land in ways that are not always economically productive or socially responsible. It cannot be simply assumed that secure and free title will automatically lead to the attainment of the most optimum use of land resources. There has, therefore, to be not only complimentary production factors but also relevant state intervention mechanisms to go along with tenure security to ensure the achievement of the best use of land. This is well in accord with the triad definition of land as 'rights, responsibilities and restraints'.

Public tenure

Public tenure involves direct ownership of land by the state; examples in Kenya include gazetted forests, national parks, urban centres and other alienated or unalienated government land. Public tenure is really individual tenure; the only difference being that the state is the owner and, often times functions as the landlord.

Urban land leaseholds

The policy for land in Kenya's urban areas is that land is essentially owned by the state but leased to individuals on a long-term basis (usually 99 years). Leaseholds enable the state through appropriate legislative and institutional instruments to control or limit abuse and indeed encourage optimum use of the land.

Unravelling the land question: land as shared space

Land as a multi-dimensional resource

As indicated above, land cannot be treated as if it had only one aspect or dimension. There are, e.g., the economic, the anthropological, the political and the developmental aspects of land. It is, therefore, multi-dimensional resource.

58

For policy to focus on one aspect to the exclusion of other aspects, it is unlikely to achieve its goals. The two common and broad approaches to land in society are, therefore, difficulty to isolate; one which sees land as basically a part of the social relations between people and society and the other which sees land basically as a part of the economic relations between persons and persons in society (Ghai, 1985:395-397). The former is based on an approach to society, which does not differentiate between economic and social relations in society; the economic aspects of land are part of the social relations and are all-important. Traditional society is governed by customary practices provide examples of such an approach to land; the customary laws are an outward sign, personification, of such an approach to society and land. The later, on the other hand, with regard to societies, which are dominated by market forces where economic and social relations are largely seen in isolation and land is viewed purely as a commodity. Modern statutory land law is largely designed to facilitate the operation of the market and so advance this approach to society and land. Unless, therefore, some recognition is given to both of these approaches to society and land, land policy and land reform are unlikely to be effective. The appreciation on this phenomena is perhaps more important in developing countries where a complex mixture of communal and individual rights in the use of resources is common. The concepts of land as shared space and land circuits attempts to unravel this phenomenon.

Shared space: the concept of 'circuits to land'

To understand the existence of, and consequently give recognition to, such contradictory approaches to land, the concept of 'circuits to land' has been proposed (McAuslan, 1987). The notion of circuits is taken from Milton Santos who formulated the notion of the two circuits of the urban economy in his book, *The Shared Space*. These two circuits are interrelated and overlapping. He describes them as follows:

> The upper circuit is the direct result of technological progress and its most representative elements are the monopolies. Most of its relations take place outside the city and the surrounding area and operate in a national and international framework. The lower circuits consist of small-scale activities and are almost exclusively for the poor. Unlike the upper circuit, the lower circuit is well entrenched in the city and enjoys privileged relations with its environment (Santos, 1979:10).

Santos advances this approach as a way of making sense of the urban economy of cities in developing societies with a view to arriving at policies which are realistic and which have potential for success in tackling problems of those cities, problems, which sometimes seem intractable. The fundamental point is that there are two largely different economies co-existing and overlapping in the same space, the city, and both have a role to play and policy must recognise that.

In adapting this approach to explicate the land question in general, McAuslan (1987) suggests that there are three circuits of land relations in many developing states. These circuits are, too, overlapping and often times share the same space and must be taken account of in policies. These circuits are:

- customary or communal land and its regulation via traditional processes - its space is principally but not exclusively in rural society;
- an unofficial market regulated by custom and practice - its space is principally urban and peri-urban but it is also gaining importance in the rural society; and
- the modern official land market regulated by statutory codes of law - its space is both urban and rural.

Using Santos' terms, the argument continues: the modern official land market is the upper circuit in both rural and urban sectors; customary land is the lower circuit in the rural sector and unofficial markets the lower circuit in the urban sector; and where customary and unofficial markets exist in the same space both are lower to the upper modern circuit. All the circuits are seen as fundamental to the land question:

> All the circuits are however essential not only to the general health and functioning of society but to each other; that is, there is a place for all of them in any society and any attempt to ignore or, worse, peremptorily to abolish or eliminate one circuit is likely to have unforeseen deleterious consequences on the other circuits (McAuslan, 1987:8).

The overlapped nature of land circuits: basis for land policy

To understand the place of land in a developing society is therefore to recognise the existence of the three overlapping and interrelated sets of land relations or circuits in society. These sets of relations or circuits are seen as overlapping in two senses. Firstly, people move between the circuits both in terms of their actual relationship to land and the transactions they engage in (e.g., a person may both own and deal in the upper circuit in town and have rights and duties in respect of customary land in the lower circuit in his or her rural village of origin) and in terms of their assumptions about relationships to land (e.g., a formal transaction in the upper circuit may be infused with notions about or contain elements or rights and duties derived from the lowest circuit). Secondly, it may be difficult to determine whether a particular piece of land is within a particular circuit; it may well be within more than one circuit, each circuit giving rise to its own set of rights and duties. The case of squatter settlements illustrates this issue. In this case, urban land in the upper or third circuit is occupied and dealt with in accordance with the norms of, and brought within the, lower or second circuit. As McAuslan says:

> each circuit is, in the eyes of its users, legitimate; each circuit is integral part of the whole society and one cannot make assumptions about legality or illegality, legitimacy or illegitimacy of any circuit (1987:9).

In the case of Kenya, where a variety of land tenures, including a continuum cutting across the three land tenure and related circuits, co-exist along one another and sometimes in the same space or real property, this framework of perceiving land and the related relations becomes quite instructive.

Against the background of the three circuits of land relations, and given the justification for state intervention or involvement in the circuits and the land question, and having briefly thrown some light on both the land tenure/relations and related control and management issues, what then are the general indications as to what should be the components of a viable land policy?

Land policy in circuit one: the traditional sector

The basis of land policy in this circuit is the recognition that a large part of Kenyan citizens are small-scale and peasant farmers and pastoralists and a big part of urban residents live in squatter and informal settlements. Traditional or customary laws and practices largely govern their relationship to the land. Land relations in this circuit provide both a living and way of life for many Kenyans and cannot therefore be neglected or relegated to the status of second class. A land policy based on the five suggested components gives recognition of this important sector of the land and economic relations. For example, the recognition of the different components point us in the direction of an acceptance of the continued existence of customary land relations; efficiency and equity point us in the direction of devising land policies which assist in the more or enhanced beneficial use customary land so as to increase its economic worth (productive output) and its social utility (more persons to have stake in the land and society); and the protection of the national patrimony point us to devising land policies which would enhance the protection and enhancement of the quality and usefulness of land by discouraging 'bad' and encouraging 'good' land use.

There is an important aspect of equity - pursuit of just and fair policies - that should apply to land policy in circuit one; this would apply equally to policies in circuit two. This is related to the question of community participation. Policies cannot, if they are to aspire to fairness and justice, be laid down from on high or the top; there must be a commitment to work with the people; policies must be a co-operative effort that harnesses the knowledge, enthusiasm and experience of the people living within circuits one and two while at the same time utilising the professionals and experts from outside the circuits to produce land policies which have more chance of being effective because they have the support of the beneficiaries. Group and co-operative land tenure arrangements in urban and rural Kenya are good examples of dealing with a complex land relationship phenomena that would otherwise created immense undesirable social and indeed economic and environmental consequences. As most of the land under this type of tenure is increasingly being broken up or miniaturised towards more individualised holdings, however, the possibility of sub-economic parcellation is becoming a reality. Undesirable environmental and ecological consequences are also becoming real, especially in the areas where either the land holding capacities are low (e.g., arid and semi-arid lands of the northern, eastern and southern Kenya) or there are the complex people-animal-wildlife land relationships (e.g., the areas in Maasailand which are part of the national parks and wildlife reserves).

In summary, desirable policies in circuit one must be developed in a way similar to and indeed must be a major part of integrated rural development planning, whose purpose is to revive and transform the agricultural and rural community by a concerted programme development on all fronts - economic, social, agricultural, rural industry, the role of women, customary law and practices, etc. With regard to land policies in circuit one, the starting point should be the reality of land relations as social relations; to work with rather than against the grain; to develop land relations from the bottom up and from within rather than from the top down and from without, recognising the validity and usefulness of much of what occurs now, rather than assuming that it has no merit and needs to be swept away. Some of the land relations in this circuit have survived for very long without endangering or unduly destroying the socio-cultural, economic and environmental base of the communities. The taping of such indigenous and traditional knowledge may be the only viable way to safe such areas from unwarranted under-development.

Land policy in circuit two: the informal and transitional zone

Circuit two is the intermediate circuit, it straddles both rural and urban society and it contains within itself aspects of both of circuit one - communal or customary rights in land - and circuit three - individualised and market relations. The classic situation in circuit two occurs in both rural and urban contexts where a market in land exists yet official law governing land markets are ignored, not out of any deliberate policy of flouting that law but because it just does not cater for the needs of people within the circuit. There exists, for example, in the both urban public and private land and registered areas in rural areas the existence of an unofficial land market where land is bought and sold, sub-divided, occupied under agreements, etc., without reference to official land and both formal urban and agricultural management laws and procedures. Officials' knowledge over the state of affairs on the ground is slight. In urban squatter settlements or unauthorised or popular housing, definition and application of official urban land law and planning requirements are non-existent. In the eyes of the law and official government circles, the occupation of the land is 'illegal' (yet settlement and land development go on anyway) or the land may be owned legally but the developments or superstructures are 'illegal' or 'unauthorised'. In both cases people within such developments engage in transactions in the real property. Such markets have been variously referred to as 'pirate subdivisions', 'illegal colonies', 'slum real estate', etc. (Kiamba, 1991a, 1992; Kiamba *et al,* 1992).

The land relationship situation confronting land policy makers in circuit two therefore is quite different from that which confronts them in circuit one or three. The situation is basically one of formal illegality - land relations permeating throughout a defined group in society giving rise to mutual rights and obligations within that group yet unsupported by the formal legal and governmental system. Which way, e.g., should land policy go - to recognise and work 'with' the illegal land occupiers and developers or to assert the formal legal system 'against' the squatters? The hitherto discussed five components of land policy and the concept of the three circuits - each equally entitled to be judged on its merits by the organs of the state - are aimed at explaining the content of land policy. The reality is that people are using land for homes, for food production, for industrial and commercial enterprise, as a source of income and livelihood, often as a substitute for a state operative social security system. The approach therefore should be to provide support - expertise, materials, a relevant and desirable legal and administrative framework, finance and land - for the initiative and enterprise already being shown by the people of the second circuit. Here, like in the first circuit, policy initiatives must be developed in partnership with the people and adopt integrated approach - a concerted programme of urban development and rural development designed to affect and improve all aspects of the lives of the people of this circuit.

Land policy in circuit three: the modern and formal sector

The third circuit is the so called 'modern' or 'formal' circuit; the one where land relations are regulated by formal structures, including legislation and judicial decisions, government administrative institutions and mechanisms and professionals advice. This is the area of predominantly individual or private landed property. Land within this circuit in Kenya is strictly confined to urban centres and commercial agricultural areas. Beyond these areas, the third circuit begins to shade into the second circuit, for example, where land reform carried out in the 1950s and 1960s with land transferred from customary to statutory titles and thereafter regulated under the Registered Land Act of 1963, is slowly slipping back into a quasi-customary regime as traditional patterns of succession to land begin to reassert themselves. Although the amount of land involved in the third circuit may be small, its economic and social importance is great. Just as in colonial times the large landowners had disproportionate political and economic power, so now large landowners in the cities and rural Kenya can drive up the price of land, of food, of housing, use their landholding to enhance their political power. By the same token, the allocation of public land within this circuit has become an important factor in Kenya's political influence and patronage.

The aims and content of land policy for the third circuit are different from the first and second circuit. The policies normally will depend on whether the focus is on the issues of the right to use land ('ius utendi'), the right to benefit from the fruits of land ('ius fruendi'), or the right to dispose of land ('ius abutendi'). The broad objective in the first category, the right to use land, is to guide and support, and to provide facilities for the better use of land. The policy while not inhibiting the profitable use and development of land, ought to ensure that the externalities of that profitable use and development are properly considered before development commences; i.e., the social and community costs and benefits are weighed as well as the private benefits to the developer. This is the area also where the formal and statutory planning and development control is possible.

Land policy at the second category, the right to benefit from the fruits of land, is in the heart of the landlord/tenant relationship; the focus here is to deal with equity perspective of the inequalities inherent in that relationship whether in the agricultural or the urban sector. Policy should ensure that bargains between landlord and tenant are fair and provide, within framework of certainty, for the efficient and equitable use of land. The policy in this area also should deal with that analogous relationship to landlord and tenant, i.e., the relationship of the mortgagee and mortgagor; analogous because of inequality of bargaining power between the supplier of the desired commodity - land in the case of landlord, finance in the case of mortgagee - and the would-be consumer. The policy, here too, needs to focus on ensuring that mortgage bargains are fair. Policy in the third category, the right to dispose of land, has focused on the need for efficiency and certainty in the operation of the market for land.

Realism and institutional innovations in land tenure strategies

Introduction

Considered below are some examples of still evolving, or embryonic, responses to the challenging land tenure question. These approaches, once again, go beyond conventional shibboleths and paradigms in order to respond positively and innovatively to the challenges.

Government as a facilitator: governance and the enabling institutional building

The emergence of non-traditional or alternative organisational forms of governance has been against the background of the debate between the notions of 'government' and 'governance'. Although these terms have sometimes been regarded and used interchangeably, it is being realised that they have important conceptual differences. As defined in some on-going researches, for example on governance without government (Young and von Moltke, 1994), governments are organisational constructs or material entities that are too often infused with powerful political ideologies and usually stalled in bureaucratic paralysis, political gridlock, environmental degradation and, sometimes, the repression of human rights. Governance on the other hand, implies a broader social act that call on a variety of agents and values to deal with the fierce demands of issues and global interdependence. It concerns the management of complex interdependencies among many different actors - individuals, corporations, interest groups, nations states - involved in interactive decision-making that affect each other's welfare. Clearly, this is the optimum scenario for what has come to be called an enabling environment.

As the UNDP's 'Human Development Report' aptly observes when discussing the imperative of 'new forms of national and local governance', when people organise, by definition they increase their level of participation and often increase influence over their own lives (UNDP, 1993). It points out that the dramatic shift towards democracy across the developing world has led to an explosion of participatory movements and NGOs. The expansion of NGO activity has been supported by aid donors who, apparently dissatisfied with the performance of much of the official aid that has been provided, are channelling more of their money in this direction. Stressed is the variety of roles performed by NGOs including the promotion of democracy, reaching the poorest of the society in circumstances where governments have been unable to do so and helping to empower marginalised groups.

Against this backdrop, Kenya has not been left behind in the search for and experimentation with fresh, perhaps unconventional but workable forms of governance for land and housing for the poor and generally in the development arena of human settlements. The aim has generally been the encouragement of an enabling governance strategy that underscores the taping, harnessing and facilitation of creativity, initiatives and energies of individuals, communities and businesses in land and shelter strategies.

To harness these resources it has been has necessary to perceive the government as a facilitator of individual and/or private initiatives by creating land policies and intervention strategies that encourage and facilitate individuals to have access to a reasonable secure land. The attempts or intervention strategies appear to be organised around an accepted relationship of partnership between the government and private individuals. Each part plays the role or roles, which they are best placed to play. In this connection, government's role is now increasingly understood as less on controlling the supply and more in setting the framework to encourage and support land markets that can respond to the variety of demands from different individuals, households, enterprises, and investors. Government and the local authorities, therefore, are reduced to the roles of providing the land (including its security of tenure), basic infrastructural and community facilities and legal and institutional framework upon which individuals and private firms move in to undertake relevant development.

Land markets can only function effectively if they are characterised by ease of entry and ease of buying and selling - which in turn depends on a good information system about land, including who owns and has right to what plot, secure tenure arrangements and appropriate registration and recording mechanisms (Farvacgue and McAuslan, 1992).

In looking at these alternative forms of governance, a caution is important. The growth of, e.g., NGOs and their impact can obscure the fact that they still operate on a relatively small scale. The argument is that NGOs can supplement the role of governments, but they can never replace it - hence the emphasis on partnerships and co-operation rather than replacement or antagonistic relations in the emerging new and alternative forms of governance.

Granting of secure land tenure

The lands on which informal and squatter settlements occur belong to the government of private parties. Squatters can readily be displaced in if the authorities or private owners choose. It seems quite clear that security of tenure is a key ingredient in self-improvement of informal sector areas. With a long-term secure interest in the shelter unit and in site, people will devote resources to improve their dwellings and living environments. Without secure tenure, however, this commitment of energies and resources is not likely to occur. As long as residents of squatter settlements face the threat of eviction, they will be unwilling to invest in their homes. Many approaches to tenure are being tried, from outright grants of ownership to various forms of long-term lease on the land or shelter unit allowing ultimate ownership to remain with the state. Such leasehold arrangements also permit the opportunity for eventual redevelopment of such neighbourhoods if the prospects for more conventional shelter solutions improve over time.

Squatter/settlement upgrading

The upgrading approach recognises that displacement and/or eviction of squatters and elimination of the informal sector are 'non-win' situations. Displacement merely shifts the shelter burden to other areas. Upgrading involves the improvement of squatter and/or low-income unplanned settlement in largely two ways:

- regularisation or improving the security of land tenure, i.e., the squatters or residents of the settlements receive a form of title for the plot they occupy; and
- basic improvement or servicing of the settlement, i.e., the settlement is provided with basic infrastructure and services.

The improvement of the houses is normally left to the residents themselves, and the improved security of the tenure is expected to be a sufficient incentive for them to invest in the improvement of their houses.

There is the need to strike a careful balance between the form of tenure and improvement. Where as in many upgrading programmes improved tenure security is an explicit goal, ironically, tenure security can result in less real security for initial beneficiaries and tenants and other very low-income households in the settlement. The resulting security of tenure increases both marketability and attractiveness of the land and improvements and, hence may facilitate middle-income groups buying out poorer families in a process known variously as 'buying out', 'downward raiding', or 'involuntary downward filtering'. Higher income 'raiders' displace original squatter-owners and tenants and others in an act of involuntary upward filtering (or, perhaps, gentrification), or buy others in voluntary transactions, which nonetheless, comprises the filtering process. The policy question would thus be whether or not upward filtering belies the officially stated objectives of settlement upgrading, and, if it does, whether it possible to limit it (upward filtering).

In this connection, the subsequent question would be what are the strategies that may be utilised in limiting the process? Would, for example, the 'rationalisation' and/or 'security' of land tenure in squatter settlements simply mean granting of outright freehold (or absolute proprietorship) or some form of leasehold or other form of terminable interest or group interest (e.g., community trust) in upgraded settlements. Although security of tenure is certainly important in the encouragement of improvements, the crucial question is what appropriate form of tenure that would invite improvements without granting so much that the upgraded property becomes a speculation commodity - hence leading to involuntary filtering of the poor and other disadvantaged groups in the society.

Various forms of site and services and self-help solutions

Governments have increasingly recognised that upgrading or improvement can help poor urban residents, but further, bolder, and more non-conventional solutions are essential to accommodate new housing demand. The response has been to assemble land in newly developing sections of the city, to divide the land into regularised plots, to provide basic infrastructure, and to grant tenure through various leasehold arrangements. Forms of actual shelter construction on these sites range from completely self-built units, almost total in character, to more urban kind of dwellings involving both contractor and family labour. Often these plot allocations have been combined with special long-time financing arrangements for the shelter unit for building materials.

The site and service development provides plots with cither full service infrastructure, consisting of, for example, earth roads and storm water drainage. The latter type would eventually be upgraded to full service provision once population densities warrant the additional investment. This kind of development has normally been on public land and its beneficiaries are specifically targeted households generally within the middle-income and low-income groups. Examples of this approach have formed an important component of urban project co-funded by the Kenya Government and the World Bank Group including projects such as the 'First Urban Project' (Dandora Community Project) in Nairobi, the 'Second Urban Project' (Mathare Valley North, Dandora Area 6 and Kayole in Nairobi, Chaani, Miritini and Mikindani in Mombasa), and the 'Third Urban Project' or 'Secondary Towns Project' (including schemes such as Racetrack in Nakuru, Kiwara/Shauri Yako and Kigongo in Nyeri and Kipkaren on Old Uganda Road in Eldoret).

Community land ownership

An approach which is starting to gain renewed acceptance in Kenya is the concept of community land ownership where the title to the land and infrastructure is held by a community unit or corporate entity (in which all the participants would own a share) with individual tenure applying to the buildings and other improvements. It is this concept that has been applied in 'horizontal properties' (e.g., condominiums) co-operative, 'shared-time, community land trust developments' and 'group ranches'.

Servicing of unoccupied private land

The servicing of unoccupied private land is a project type is geared towards pre-empting the situation that has developed in most of the urban fringe land in Kenya. Much of the lands have been purchased by land companies and co-operatives societies. Once the land is formally subdivided among the company and co-operative members and occupied, the land title situation quickly becomes confused with the result that future planning, infrastructure provision and development control of the land is very difficult. Coupled with this lending institutions are not well geared to provide funds for individual private developers to install infrastructure services, particularly at the standard of servicing affordable by the low-income residents. The project, therefore, is to attempt to avoid this problem by involving local authorities in servicing large tracts of mainly unoccupied private land as a basis for future urban growth. The costs of the infrastructure would be recovered from the landowners through a combination of road charges, public utility charges and land taxes development. Control would be exercised through normal planning regulations and building by-laws applicable in such areas.

Linking land to infrastructure and income generation

In all the above approaches, two common characteristics are evident:

- they provide crucial linkage between land and the provision of infrastructure and development. The most effective institutional initiatives encompass land as a component of the development process, intimately tied with other components of urbanisation. They do not treat land in isolation. In this connection land is linked to the provision of infrastructure and appropriate use;
- increasing the supply of affordable land within reach of appropriate employment and income generating opportunities or relevant economic activities. The basis of this approach is that housing and employment linkage is crucial to the community as both consumers and producers - extended journey-to-work are unproductive, costly and make extraordinary demands on public resources and the environment. Without due regard to the incorporation of income-generating opportunities into land and shelter projects meant to help the poor will come to nought.

These emerging approaches to the provision of land and housing to the poor in developing countries are clearly fundamental in successful urban management.

Socio-economic groupings and self-help as tools for development

Social and economic oriented groups are an important vehicle/tool for community and development activities in poor communities. Groups are seen as important tool in the self-organisation and mobilisation of the community around simple and immediate or urgent felt need. Being organised on the basis of collective self-help, they are a vital focus of communal consensus and also self-awareness and neighbourhood spirit. They are normally small scale, and tend to have simple and clearly defined agenda and participation arrangements, including determination of legitimate and accountable officials or leadership of the group. These socio-economic groups are the basis for innovative land tenurial arrangements like community land trusts, co-operative land systems, group land ownership systems, etc.

Gender sensitivity: women's role in land ownership, use and development

In most poor settlements in the urban areas in Kenya, women make the greater proportion of the head of households. This has implications on strategies for land and shelter provision. For example, in Kitui-Pumwani settlement in Nairobi, women households amount to between 75% and 80% of the total heads of households (Kiamba *et al*, 1992). Women were often present in the settlements as they managed rental rooms and water kiosks and small-scale informal businesses. Women are not only more present in the settlements but also more seriously affected by the lack of services such as decent housing, water and sanitation as are normally responsible for collecting water and disposing off household waste. Clearly, women have more to gain from improved services in the community and are therefore more motivated and receptive to involvement in community and self-help development activities that ensure their continued provision. Its no wonder that women in Kitui-Pumwani form the largest number of CBOs, ranging from water groups, house building groups, social and cultural groups. They therefore are natural target group for NGOs that are interested in initiating community based and managed projects. As a most important force in such settlements, women as a social group, therefore form an important target for any viable strategies for land and shelter development.

In many developing countries, women's capacity to acquire, own, manage and develop land is affected not only by prevailing social customs determining gender relations within household and community, but also their lack of access to credit, technical support, infrastructure, education and their exclusion from governance and other decision making bodies. The prevalence of custom over law, the existence of silent and unspoken sanctions, the lack of gender-aware government policies and ignorance of rights militate against women and poor communities' capacity to actualise their rights. In Kenya, using access to both urban and rural land, including informally allocated plots, Lee-Smith found out that three-quarters of urban women heading households were landless compared to 35% of the urban poor as a whole:

> It appears conclusive that women are disadvantaged as compared to men (1995:56).

'Secure access' to land is not to be seen just as a mere ownership of the land but also a more complex social process including 'usufructuary' rights like situations where women have access to land in stable marriage environments.

For land tenure policy and strategies, therefore, to increase their positive mediating capacity in development, they must be gender sensitive. They must guarantee women's rights to land, including right to inherit, own, use and convey and dispose of property according to the law on an equitable basis with men without discrimination. In this regard, the gender equity as fair balance in the rapidly changing social relations between men and women will have been advanced.

Conclusion

What has been attempted in this paper is a brief and general overview of evolving approaches to land tenure arrangements to improve land development processes (and especially land and housing conditions of those who live in poverty and disadvantaged circumstances) and to suggest that a review of 'conventional wisdom' may be in order.

The circumstances that existed in the 1960s and 1970s in Kenya, on which conventional wisdom was based on, are now different. The problem in Kenya, typical of many countries in the developing world, is that urbanisation and social change has been occurring at such unprecedented rapid rates that it has been difficulty or impossible for institutional adjustments to keep pace. The rapid and apparently inexorable tightening of land availability combined with consolidation of control over supply present a lot of challenges for now and in the future. Responding to these challenges is important because they increasingly diminish opportunities for low-income families, raise costs and complicate the administration of land development and urban management strategies.

There is the need for new or at least innovative forms of land tenure to be invented in order to serve the new social needs more realistically. It is imperative, at any rate, to make conceptionalisation of the solutions of change at least as rapidly as the fast changing urban scenario. Kenya, in its own unique way, must invent a paradigm of land tenure that optimises efficiency and effectiveness while maintaining enough equity to keep the society stable.

References

Angel, S., 1983a. Upgrading slum infrastructure: divergent objectives in search of consensus, *Third World Planning Review*, **5**, 5-22.

Angel, S., 1983b. Land tenure for the urban poor. In: Angel, S., *et al* (eds.) *Land for housing the poor,* Select Books, Singapore.

Burgess, R., 1985. The limits of state self-help housing programmes, *Development and Change*, **16**, 271-312.

Burgess, R., 1987. A lot of noise and no nuts: a reply to Alan Gilbert and Jan van Linden, *Development and Change*, **18**(2), 137-146.

Cloke, P.J. (ed.), 1989. *Rural Land Use Planning in Developed Nations*, Unwin Hyman, London.

Doebele, W.A., 1975. The private market and low-income urbanisation in developing countries: the 'pirate' sub-divisions of Bogota, *American Journal of Comparative Law*, **25**(3), 531-564.

Doebele, W.A., 1983. Concepts of urban land tenure. In: Dunkerley, H.B. (ed.), *Urban land policy: Issues and opportunities,* Oxford University Press, New York, USA, 63-107.

Doebele, W.A., 1987. The evolution of concepts of urban land tenure in developing countries, *Habitat International*, **11**(1), 2-22.

Farvacque, C. & McAuslan, P., 1992. *Reforming Urban Policies and Institutions in Developing Countries,* Urban Management Programme Policy Paper No. 5, The World Bank, Washington, DC.

Ghai, Y.P., 1985. Land regimes and paradigms of development: reflections on Melanesian Constitutions, *International Journal of Sociology and Law*, **13**.

Gilbert, A. & Ward, P., 1982. Low income and the state, *Urbanisation in Contemporary Latin America,* John Wiley & Sons, Chichester, UK.

Gilbert, A. & Ward, P., 1985. *Housing, the state and the poor: Policies and practice in three Latin America cities,* Cambridge University Press, Cambridge, UK.

Government of Kenya (GOK), 1986. *Economic Management with Renewed Growth,* Sessional Paper No. 1 of 1986, Government Printer, Nairobi.

Harvey, D., 1982. *Limits of Capital*, Basil Blackwell, Oxford, UK.

Kiamba, M., 1986. *The Role State in the Control of Urban Development: Urban Land Policy for Nairobi, Kenya*, Ph.D dissertation, University of Cambridge, Cambridge.

Kiamba, M., 1989. The introduction and evolution of private landed property in Kenya, *Development and Change*, **20**, 121-147.

Kiamba, M., 1991a. Some squatter/settlement upgrading issues and policy in Kenya. Paper presented at the *Workshop on Squatter/Settlement Upgrading in Kenya*, organised by the Department of Land Development, University of Nairobi, Mombasa.

Kiamba, M., 1991b. Overview of Kenya's urban development policy, *Review of Rural and Urban Planning in Southern and Eastern Africa*, **1**, 93-100.

Kiamba, M. 1992. Regeneration of low-income housing and squatter settlement areas in Nairobi, Kenya: partnership relation between state and private capital. In: Kilmartin, L. & Singh, H. (eds.), *Housing in the Third World: Analysis and Solutions*, Concept Publishing Company, New Delhi, India.

Kiamba, M., *et al*, 1992. *Urban Management Instruments for Neighbourhood Development in Selected African Cities: The Kenya Case*, Research Project Paper, Department of Land Development, University of Nairobi.

Kiamba, M., 1994a. The dynamics of urbanisation and urban development policy in Kenya. In: Wekwete, K.H. & Rambanapasi, C.O. (eds.), *Planning urban economies in Southern and Eastern Africa*, Avebury, Aldershot, UK.

Kiamba, M. 1994b. The primacy of land in rural development: issues and options in Kenya, *Review of Rural and Urban Planning in Southern and Eastern Africa*, **1**, 32-51.

Lee-Smith, D. 1995. Women's and men's rights to and control of land and property in Eastern Africa. Paper presented at the International Workshop on *Women's Access, Control and Tenure of Land, Property and Settlement*, held at Gävle, Sweden.

Massey, D. & Catalano, A., 1978. *Capital and Land*, Edward Arnold, London, UK.

Mather, A.S., 1986. *Land Use*, Longman, London, UK.

McAuslan, P., 1985. *Urban Land and Shelter for the Poor*, Earthscan, London, UK.

McAuslan, P., 1987. Land policy: a framework for analysis and action. Paper presented in a Lecture, Faculty of Law, University of Lagos, Nigeria.

McLaughlin, J., 1981. *Notes and materials for cadastral studies*, Department of Surveying Engineering, University of New Brunswick, Canada.

Okoth-Ogendo, H.W.O., 1991. *Tenants of the Crown*, ACTS Press, Nairobi, Kenya.

Payne, G.K., 1982. Self-help housing: a critique of the 'Gecekondus' of Ankara. In: Ward, P.M. (ed.), *Self-help housing: A critique*, London, UK.

Santos, M., 1979. *The Shared Space*, London, UK.

Sarin, M., 1983. The rich, the poor and the land question. In: Angel S., *et al* (eds.), *Land for Housing the Poor*, Select Books, Singapore.

Thirkell, A.J., 1996. Players in urban informal land markets; who wins, who loses? A case study of Cebu City, *Environment and Urbanisation*, **8**(2), 71-90.

Varley, A., 1987. The relationship between tenure legalisation and housing improvements: evidence from Mexico City, *Development and Change*, **18**, 463-481.

Wegelin, E.A. & Chanond, C., 1983. Home improvement, housing finance and security of tenure in Bangkok slums. In: Angel, S. *et al* (eds.), *Land for Housing the Poor*, Select Books, Singapore.

World Bank, 1993. *Housing: Enabling Markets to Work*, Washington, DC, USA.

Young, O.R. & von Moltke, 1993. To gridlock: governance without government, *The United Nations Work in Progress*, **14**(2), 5.

Sustainable spatial development of the coastline of England and Wales

Robert W. DIXON-GOUGH
Land Management Research Unit, School of Surveying, University of East London

Abstract

This paper addresses three main issues: the importance of sustainability, particularly within the context of the legislation of England and Wales; the concept of sustainability as applied to the coastline of England and Wales and introduces some concepts of inter-disciplinary co-operation in the quest for sustainable coastal management strategies; and finally presents some case studies that involve a high level of interdisciplinary co-operation.

One of the aspects to be investigated in this paper is the hypothesis that our concept of sustainability has changed and will change in the future. This paper examines the debate concerning sustainability from the context of the coastline of England and Wales, and in particular the environmental problems caused by an unsustainable use of coastal resources. One of the most fundamental reasons for environmental problems, particularly in coastal regions, is poor or inappropriate land management practice. The debate and implementation of any form of sustainable development can viewed from two opposing aspects: the debate from a top-down approach, whilst the implementation is often at a local level. This paper will examine the need for partnership arrangements to exploit and organise the complex issues that often arise, particularly in coastal regions.

Introduction

The definition of sustainability as cited in many dictionaries is 'to uphold, to maintain or to keep'. To many, this definition implies a quality that denotes of form of status quo that has to be maintained, such as a means of preventing or minimising change. Traditionally, it would have defined a more settled way of life and, in many respects, the ability of the human race (or tribe or group) to survive in a natural environment. As civilisations developed, location-specific activities such as arable farming, settlements, the development of industries, commerce and trade, and communication links became more important and large sections of the community lost their direct relationship to the land. Thus social communities became larger and more structured and power, particularly expressed in land ownership, became very important.

Historically, and in relatively simple societies and economies, resources have been subconsciously used in a sustainable manner. The most important assets such as grazing land, woodland, water supplies and areas for fishing have been held as common property resources (Berkes, 1989). In England and Wales, there are still a few areas of 'common land', upon which certain specified commoners (the title to which, normally being attached to the deeds of a property on or adjacent to the common land) are permitted to exercise certain rights. These are typically rights of access, to gather fallen timber and to graze animals. In addition *de facto* public access rights may exist. In the case of common land for example, the New Forest in Central Southern England, a committee representing the various users normally takes collective decisions.

However, the definition and concept of sustainability is now changing to encompass our way of life and the ways in which our actions today may affect the life styles and health of future generations. The most familiar interpretation and most widely accepted current definition and concept of sustainable use, is that defined by the World Commission on Environment and Development (1987) - the so-called Brundtland report, which defined sustainability as being a process:

> that meets the needs of the needs of the present without compromising the ability of future generations to meet their own needs.

It is this definition and concept of sustainability that will be explored in the context of this paper.

The context of sustainability

This is not one that lends itself to many traditional or recently practised forms of land management. The purpose of this paper is not to discuss *per se* the truth of sustainability but to examine how the context of

78

sustainability must be embedded within the general context of land management and the more specific context of coastal zone management.

One of the problems of sustainability is that it is a very difficult concept to define and explain in specific terms. Here, we may compare the concept of planning for sustainability and planning for development purposes. Sustainable development may be characterised as being more *idealistic, holistic* and *radical*, whilst development planning was seen as more *pragmatic, sectoral* and *revisionist*. This problem is exacerbated by the apparent confusion of many experts such as land managers and land administrators, rural and urban planners, environmentalists and environmental economists. For example, Counsell (1999) considers that sustainable development is often considered as a theoretical concept that should be discussed in abstract terms. The translation of that abstract idea into operational practice gives rise to problems both to the lack of understanding about what sustainable development means and, very significantly, because it appears to mean different things to different people (Torgerson, 1995; Mitlin and Satherthwaite, 1995). For example, Dixon-Gough (1999) suggests that the sustainable development of an urban area might imply the continued economic growth of that area. Similarly, it has been argued by many environmental economists (Selman, 1992) that sustainability should be capable of being achieved through a trade-off between the interests of resource consumption on one-hand, and the environmental quality on the other. This ideal cannot, however, be satisfactorily achieved in practise since market failures can arise in many different ways and inevitably results in some form of unsustainable failure.

In terms of application, the majority of operational concepts of sustainable development involve a resource protection model, where it is envisaged that the capital stock (involving natural and human assets) is handed on to future generations without reduction. The composition of this stock, and in particular the way in which the critical natural stock is dealt with, determines the strength of usage (Owens, 1994). Thus, those promoting the concepts of sustainable development need to indicate the need for a high level of integration between land use planning and the wider social, economic and environmental considerations (Blowers, 1993; Lusser, 1993).

However, the institutional constraints in the planning system of England and Wales largely prevent the development of appropriate planning policies. Blowers (1992) has suggested that the current planning system in England and Wales needs to be replaced by a more comprehensive means of environmental management that takes into account the trans-media, trans-sectional and trans-boundary nature of environmental processes. This is particularly true when many of the local decisions that have to be made relate to the global economy, in which local decision-makers have to contend with multinational or national organisations. Those organisations are far more likely to seek short-term economic and, even, political interests than to take a long-term assessment of the situation (Garner, 1996; Taussik, 1997).

Hales (2000) identifies the five key application principles for sustainable knowledge as:

- *the precautionary principle*, which places the burden of proof in decision-making on establishing that valued socio-environmental resources are protected in instances of uncertainty over the impacts of development;
- *environmental thresholds/limits*, which involves the making of specific judgements about the valued socio-environmental resources to accept demands upon them without irreversible of otherwise acceptable loss or damage, or set limits/thresholds for development beyond which demand could no longer be met without resulting in irreversible loss or damage;
- *environmental compensation*, which requires compensatory measures for any loss of socio-environmental value, caused by a result of development activity, with commensurate socio-environmental benefits;
- *demand management*, which is a development activity, regulated so as to modify forecasted demand rather than simply accommodating it, on the grounds of modifying or improving socio-environmental benefits;
- *the best practicable environmental option*, in which demand for development is met whilst applying performance standards to minimise socio-environmental degradation.

From these key principles, it should be possible to develop a strategy that will involve expert knowledge, application, and a level of co-operation between the many disciplines that are involved in land and coastal management. It is the links between strategy, knowledge, application, co-operation and the many elements of socio-economic, political, cultural and physical contexts in which they may make connections (McManus, 1996), which gives sustainable development its qualities of contestability and indeterminacy. Contestability and indeterminacy should not, however, be perceived as weaknesses. These factors are the hallmarks of possibility and choice (Torgerson, 1995) and it through these variables that inter-disciplinary co-operation should be allowed to flourish.

The elements of possibility and choice lead to three questions:

- What are the essential elements and characteristics of the natural and built environment?
- Who should make the decision and how should it be made?
- How is an appropriate level to be achieved?

These questions are placed in context in Figure 1, which outlines their interrelationship within the planning system of England and Wales.

When considered in the context of development planning, Wilson (1998) identifies many restraining factors over sustainable development's influence on the planning system. These include that:

- historically, the environment has been evaluated predominantly in terms of amenity, aesthetics and as a back-cloth to development;
- temporal horizons for development plans are relatively short;
- many issues are considered within a highly parochial context;
- decision-making has conventionally been biased towards a presumption in favour of development;
- land use planning is a notably sectoral activity with socio-economic and ecological needs being determined outside the planning process.

One of the problems associated with land use and development planning in England and Wales is that they normally apply to a relatively short timeframe. There are many justifications that this timeframe should be extended to between 25-30 years. Selman (1992) argues that sustainability stresses the need to view environmental protection over a longer term and that continuing economic growth should be mutually compatible activities and not necessarily conflicting ones. It implies therefore that development programmes should be consistent with the natural base limitations (Turner, 1988). Within the highly modified environments of Western Europe it is possible to distinguish between:

- productive sustainability - the use of an area's natural resources, such as soil and water, such that their long-term productivity is not impaired;
- aesthetic sustainability - the maintenance of an area's natural and cultural heritage; and
- socio-economic sustainability - the establishment of an economically viable community within an area (O'Riordan, 1983; Kirkless Metropolitan District Council, 1989; DoE, 1994).

These three forms of sustainability are all equally important within the coastal environment and it is, therefore, pertinent that the concepts and context of sustainability within coastal zone management is considered.

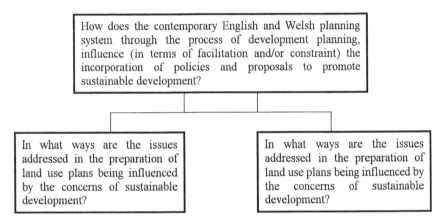

Figure 1 The hallmarks of possibility and choice with the planning system of England and Wales

Sustainability within the coastal zone

Although there are conceptual problems relating to the context and generally abstract nature of sustainability, it is possible to define more closely its' more fundamental objectives. It is generally accepted that together with riparian zones, wetlands and rainforests, the coastal zone is one of the most fragile environments. Attention was drawn forcibly to this when the Organisation for Economic Co-operation and Development (1993) called for action to further the sustainability of coastal zones, which included:

82

- the definition of policy objectives that are specific to coasts and their resources;
- the integration and harmonisation of sectoral responsibilities;
- the collection of relevant information and development of coastal environmental indices;
- public education and participation in decision-making at an early stage of policy formation; and
- the identification and testing of the relative effectiveness of different policy instruments and organisational arrangements.

This theme was given further expression by the World Coast Conference (1993) in defining an objective of integrated coastal zone management as:

> a continuous and evolutionary process for achieving sustainable development, involving the comprehensive assessment, setting of objectives, planning and management of coastal systems and resources, taking into account traditional, cultural and historical perspectives and conflicting interests and uses.

More recently, Davos (1998) suggested that the inclusion of sustainable development within coastal zone policies must be socially constructed and involve the greatest level of voluntary co-operation between stakeholders with possibly competing interests and priorities. The defining concept of a co-operative coastal zone management structure is its reliance upon the social discourse and on the framework for guiding this social discourse through the integration of diverse and conflicting interests into co-operative collective decisions. These are defined as ones that can:

- draw maximum support; and
- enhance the stakeholders' willingness to voluntarily co-operate in their implementation by inviting respect for the whole process of their selection and implementation.

This effectively emphasises the need for both inter-disciplinary co-operation and the involvement of private individuals with an interest and commitment to the coastal zone.

The fundamental challenge faced by a co-operative and inter-disciplinary coastal zone management structure is to achieve a high level of 'optimism about the level of optimism' (Seabright, 1993) particularly when dealing with additional challenges relating to:

- the process of agenda setting;
- the value of discourse; and
- the challenges of information and empowerment.

As a matter of policy, efforts should be directed towards a critical investigation into the ways in which sustainable policies of coastal zone management are socially constructed and can be implemented with the sustained co-operation of stakeholders with conflicting preferences and priorities. The specific case studies dealt with below will emphasise this aspect, which cannot be understated.

The implementation of an agenda of sustainability poses major challenges for decision-makers in achieving the correct level of balance between the needs of development and conservation (Elliot, 1993; Welsh Office, 1996). It is also important to remember that the environment simultaneously serves several purposes; it is a source of raw materials, a habitat for flora, fauna and human settlement, it is an industrial location and as an amenity. A single person or organisation may own land, yet be valued by both flora and fauna as a habitat and by a number of special interest groups. If we consider coastal farmland for example, it is primarily managed for food production, but it may also be valued by others for its close proximity to the coast (walkers and tourists), its scenic beauty and as a wildlife habitat. Any intervention by a public sector agency must take into consideration the full range of issues relating to that coastal area. One approach might be to regulate intentional or accidental change (whether by depletion, pollution or improvement) to that environment's capital stock. An alternative approach might be to adjudicate between the landowner and the various interest groups, including public sector agencies who will compete for particular resources and attitudes concerning the sustainable use of those resources.

Further complications can be the result of different professions and disciplines viewing sustainability from their own, slightly different viewpoint, which result in the introduction of semantic differences. Bowers (1997) form the viewpoint of an environmental economist argues that the neo-classical approach to sustainable development depends on the meaning attached to the concepts of 'natural capital' and the possibility of valuing it. He describes natural capital as an aggregation of a wide range of disparate items, many of which cannot be given any form of monetary value. For example, there is no correct answer to the question of whether a section of a new trunk road is worth more than five sites of special scientific interest, the remains of an Iron Age field system, the sites of a Roman villa and a Civil War battlefield, not to mention the extra emission of atmospheric pollutants that might be created as the result of the new road. This argument can easily be transposed to a coastal situation such as the example of Burling Gap, discussed below. Similarly, are the coastal defences, built by the Romans in the Severn Estuary a sustainable form of land claim, an archaeological artifact to be preserved, or an example of an unsustainable process that should be removed to prevent the coastal squeeze upon inter-tidal vegetation that is being caused through rising sea levels?

Pethick (1996), from a planning perspective, suggests that for the sustainable use of the coast, change must be the primary objective to both the spatial and temporal flexibility of its component systems and management structure. The coast is a dynamic and natural system that may easily be affected by both natural and anthropogenic factors and, thus, any system of sustainable development within the coastal zone must be capable of taking into consideration these factors in response to both natural and artificial forces. This and other definitions have helped to generate a level of confusion and uncertainty amongst coastal managers, especially since some definitions relate temporal change as the converse of sustainable use, even referring to the natural processes of erosion and deposition as a form of degradation. In this respect, Pethick (1996) cites Chapter 17 of the Agenda 21 (UNCED, 1992), which states that:

> Para 17.3 Current approaches to the management of marine and coastal resources have not always proved capable of achieving sustainable development and coastal resources and the coastal environment are rapidly being *degraded and eroded* in many parts of the world.

> Para 17.29 As concerns physical destruction of coastal and marine areas......priority action should include control and *prevention of coastal erosion and siltation* due to anthropogenic factors.

He then goes on to comment that the statements raise two major issues. The first is that erosion and siltation should not be seen as a form of degradation but as a natural response to external factors that should be accepted by coastal managers who wish to achieve a strong level of sustainability.

French (1997) refers to this process as balancing the sedimentary budget, which is an on-going process of erosion and deposition. Secondly, the changes to the coastal system may be due to anthropogenic causes as well as natural, but the response of the natural coastal processes is identical in both cases and to control the natural response to change would hardly seem the correct action in a programme of sustainable development.

The response by the government to sustainable development in the coastal zone of England and Wales is largely though PPG20 – Coastal Planning (DoE, 1992) which, although supporting those principles, fails to take into account the complexity of the zone (Cullingworth and Nadin, 1997). In a report of the Environment Committee (1992), complaints were made of the lack of co-ordination among the many bodies concerned with coastal protection, planning and management. When the report was written, there were over eighty Acts, which dealt with the regulation of activities within the coastal zone and as many as 240 different government departments and agencies involved in some. There is little doubt that these must, and to some extent, have been reduced and the level of co-operation between the bodies increased, as may be seen below.

Although changes in procedures and responsibilities have been modified and improved, Turner *et al* (1998) were still able to report that there was a strong degree of overlap of responsibilities. It was suggested that coastal zone management for sustainable development must involve a more active and conciliatory approach to consultation across and between stakeholders for any given resource allocation and environmental decision-making situation. Furthermore, it was suggested that there are strong social, political and economic arguments for widening the consultative arrangements and ensuring a greater level of co-operation and participation.

One of the defining elements of sustainability within the coastal context is that when the land is developed as intensively as it is in most countries in Europe, either along the coast or in riparian zones, the problem of sustainability has a real and human dimension, which takes it far beyond the abstract and theoretical concept outlined by Counsell (1999). In coastal terms, what exactly is sustainability? Is it to attempt to sustain the land, its ownership and the property built upon the coast or is it to allow the natural processes of the coastal dynamics to take place? One such example of coastal erosion is in the Burling Gap, Sussex (Davidson, 1998). Here, a number of houses are facing destruction as the chalk cliffs erode towards them. Already the end cottage in the row was demolished in 1995 and the next cottage in line is about 10 m from the cliff edge, which is eroding at the rate of 1m per year. Environmental groups, ranging from English Nature to the Sussex Downs Conservation Board wish nature to take its course, since to protect the cliffs would be to eliminate erosion at that point, which would result in the white cliff face becoming vegetated. The National Trust who owns three of the cottages in Burling Gap supports them. However, the community formed a Burling Gap Cliff Protection Association and applied for planning permission to erect a rock revetment at the base of the cliffs to permanently halt the erosion. During the last few months, Wealden District Council granted the planning permission, although it is uncertain who will pay for the estimated £500,000 bill for the works. This *ad hoc* Association is very good example of inter-disciplinary co-operation, since it involved a number of experts ranging from through the professions, down to interested individuals. It is not, however, typical of the form of co-operation that will be described below. It is, however, typical of a pressure group that is formed to protect a particular geographical entity and there are a number of other similar locations around the coastline of England and Wales that are under threat from coastal erosion.

The European dimension

In recognition of the European dimension of the problem of addressing the issues of sustainable development within the coastal zone, the Commission proposed in 1995 to launch a three-year demonstration programme on the integrated management of its coastal zones. This was specifically aimed towards encouraging cross border and cross sectoral dialogue and concerted action, so as to facilitate the implementation of existing legislation in this area for the purpose of sustainable coastal development and management (Anon, 1996). The European Environment Agency (EEP), as part of the EU Demonstration Programme, undertook this programme.

Between 1998 and 2000, a number of reports and recommendations that had been commissioned by the EEP were published. In chronological order, the first of these was the Thematic Study F, which addressed the issues relating to the role of information in coastal zone management (Doody, *et al*, 1998). This study concluded that:

> The key to the on-going problem in relation to the nature of the information required for coastal zone management lies not so much in the provision or the

content of the information itself, but in the way it is presented to those who formulate and implement policy and take management decisions.

The second report, published in March 1999, was designed to assess and document the degree to which the sustainable management of the coast of Europe is hindered by the lack of consistency between sectoral and territorial policies, programmes and plans (Humphrey and Burbridge, 1999). After a comprehensive examination of the various national and institution plans and programmes, it concluded that:

> the demonstration projects have confirmed that there are serious inconsistencies between sectoral and territorial policies, programmes and plans and that these are failing to provide for an integrated approach to coastal management.

The report also made a number of recommendations to local initiatives and to national and EU levels.

A further report, also published in March 1999, explored the role of participation in the process of ICZM and to recommend suitable procedures and mechanisms in order to achieve improved levels of co-operation between the various parties concerned in the process (King, 1999). The report concluded that generally:

> current practice is varied and complex due to a host of local, regional, national and international factors and circumstances. Nevertheless, study results do suggest the important role that participation has to play in establishing a foundation for the improved co-ordination/concertation that is essential to ICZM.

This report is of particular interest since it records the views and attitudes of many active participants in a wide range of aspects relating to the sustainable development of the coastal zone, particularly at the local levels where the impact and the effects are at their greatest.

A fourth report was published in October 1999, which analysed the role of law at national, EC and international levels, and considered how those mechanisms could best be applied to promote sustainable coastal development, in the form of Integrated Coastal Zone Management (ICZM), within the EU (Gibson, 1999). The report examined a range of coastal zone laws outside the EU and also considered the impact of European Community and International laws on ICZM within the EU. One particular recommendation made by the report was that whatever the mechanisms chosen for use within the EU, they must be sensitive to the legal variations of each state and permit suitable approaches to be adopted by each. It concluded with the following, and very relevant, statement:

> However, the law is not an end in itself - it is a tool to facilitate the translation of policy into practice.

The final report to be discussed as part of the Pan European Demonstration Framework is that of the influence of existing EU policies on the evolution of coastal zones (IEEP, 1999). This report assesses to what extent the existing policies of the EU contribute to, or detract from, the sustainable management of coastal areas. One significant conclusion of this report is that both the Common Agricultural Policy (CAP) and the Common Fisheries Policy (CFP) have negative influences upon the biophysical environments, and hence sustainability, of the coastal areas. It also cites two other areas of concern: those of inadequate implementation by some member states, and of an inadequate co-ordination at EU level of the objectives of some policies.

These reports culminated in the publication of two communications from the Council of the European Communities concerning the implementation of Integrated Coastal Zone Management, leading to sustainable coastal development, in Europe (CEC, 2000a; CEC 2000b), which recommend the encouragement of the Strategy across all member states.

Practical levels of co-operation in England and Wales

The role of forums, partnerships and strategy frameworks for co-operative programmes of sustainable coastal development have been discussed by Dixon-Gough (2001a; 2001b) and Home (2001). Davos (1998) also promotes the concept of co-operation through partnerships as a means of providing a sustainable development of coastal zone management that reaches across all users and interested parties of the coast. These studies, related primarily to the coastal zone, can be mirrored by similar studies related to the rural environment, such as that of Scott (1998) who addresses the use of forums as a means of promoting sustainable development through the farming community of rural Wales. To emphasise the importance, context and relevance of local co-operation, a number of case studies will be described that will provide evidence of interdisciplinary approaches to the sustainable spatial development of the coastline of England and Wales. The case studies will range from non-statutory bodies, typified by the Cardigan Bay Forum and the Morecambe Bay Strategy Framework, through to the statutory plans exemplified by the Isle of Wight Shoreline Management Plan.

The work of Forums and Strategies

The concept of Forums developed during the late 1980s (Rose, 1990) and these have now become an important addition to organisational structures dealing with problems as widely ranging as coastal regions, rural land, transport and ethnic minorities. They were given increased importance with Agenda 21 applications, which linked sustainability to a local agenda (LGMB, 1994). The growth and contribution that forums have made in furthering sustainable land use and coastal policies in rural Wales is fully documented by Scott (1998).

The Cardigan Bay Forum was established in 1991 by individuals concerned about the welfare of the bottlenose dolphins within the environs of the Bay. Meetings were initially held to assess what was happening within the Bay and to consider what could be done to protect the dolphins. This process developed further as members began to gather information to assess the other threats faced by the Bay and to plan action programmes. This eventually led to the establishment of a network of bodies and agencies, who do not normally meet and co-operate, and interested individuals. It was found that through a deeper awareness of different member's problems and perspectives, a better atmosphere could be created in which to discuss complex and sometimes emotionally laden issues (Scott, 1996). The Countryside Council of Wales provided financial support and a partnership was developed with the Welsh Institute of Rural Studies, who provided office accommodation and equipment. The most significant advance in the organisation's evolution was the creation of a development plan, which was largely instrumental in securing a more representative management committee structure (Table 1) and improving and widening the membership base (Table 2).

Table 1 The management committee of the Cardigan Bay Forum

Cardigan Bay Forum: Management Committee 1995/96
Welsh Institute of Rural Studies National Trust Aberystwyth Town Council Marathon Oil Dyfed Wildlife Trust Marine Conservation Society Welsh Water Pembrokeshire Marine Protocol Friends of Cardigan bay Mid-Wales Tourism North West and North Wales Sea Fisheries Committee

Source: Scott (1996).

Table 2 The membership of Cardigan Bay Forum

Analysis of Membership of Cardigan Bay Forum - 1996
Environmental (17) Recreational/Tourism (11) Oil/Gas (7) Other industry (6) Local Authority (13) Academic/Research (12) Forums (10) Political (11) Individuals (11) Local Community (5) Others (6)
Total (109)

Source: Scott (1996).

Clearly the Forum's approach of embracing the traditional definition of a forum is reflected in an open membership approach. This range of memberships is both an advantage and a disadvantage. It is an advantage insomuch as it serves a diverse range of interest groups within the Bay but its disadvantage lies in having to manage that wide range of diverse interests. Scott (1998) identifies the main problems as those that have been exacerbated by the Forum's success. It is increasingly being asked by organisations to comment on policy documents and management plans such as Estuary Management Plans and Local Plans. As a result, the Forum is becoming more constrained and managed and the debating and information functions are becoming the primary and most successful activities. Furthermore, there has been pressure by some members of the Forum to have a greater say in the strategic vision for Cardigan Bay and this has been tempered by the inherent danger that the Forum may be used or manipulated by organisation(s) and individuals with their own agendas (Scott, 1998). The work of the Cardigan Bay Forum may be summarised as:

> encompassing the co-operation and involvement of legitimate interests to translate sustainable rhetoric into meaningful agendas [and can] be an important facilitator to enable change in organisational attitudes and policy (Scott, 1998).

The Cardigan Bay Forum has four major remits:

- *the strategic regional remit.* The Forum operates at a regional level, which is particularly relevant since it is argued that sustainable management at a regional level is imperative (Gubbay, 1994). The Forum has a membership that spans a wide range from national through to local interests and is also multi-disciplinary. Such a membership clearly indicates the value of co-operation and information dissemination at this level;
- *the information and network remit.* Questionnaires indicate that the information service is greatly valued by the membership (Scott, 1996);
- *the influencing change remit.* This is difficult to measure in real terms. However, the Forum is directly involved in a wide range of initiatives ranging from joint publications on environmental information, developing partnership approaches to improving the quality of the coast, developing codes of conduct and new research programmes largely though the efforts and funds of industrial partners (Scott, 1996);
- *the lobby for action remit.* The Forum is not a pressure group *per se* although where lobbying has occurred on behalf on its behalf, a high degree of success has been achieved. Examples

include the need for marine issues to be addressed as part of the Ceredigion Local Plan and the Wales Rural White Paper.

The future of the Cardigan Bay Forum undoubtedly lies in its potential to act as a management agent for the proposed area of conservation in Cardigan Bay. The regional approach of the Forum has shown it to be both valuable and complementary towards a sustainable coast and it is an essential organisation to provide networks, information, research, and proactive management policies.

The concept of the Forum is one that can be used throughout England and Wales but its success is largely dependant upon having a dynamic committee and membership, some form of funding, and administrative support. The major disadvantage of the Forum is that they can easily be taken over and manipulated by organisations and individuals, either to promote some form of development or to act as a very specific pressure group.

The Morecambe Bay Strategy is, in concept very similar to that of a Forum yet its remit is much wider. Essentially, the role of the Morecambe Bay Strategy is to establish a 'partnership', which encompasses a full range of interests from all around the Bay, and a 'framework', which provides a means of helping to sustain the quality of the social, economic and environmental values of the region. This is a process that attempts to take into account all legitimate activities within the Bay. In common with the work of Forums, the Morecambe Bay Strategy is not a statutory document and neither is it biased towards any particular interest group.

Work on the Morecambe Bay Strategy began in 1992, at a time when both central and local government was beginning to recognise the need for a new approach to the management of coastal regions. The central theme of the Morecambe Bay Strategy, as too was that of the Cardigan Bay Forum, was the need to improve links between organisations. This theme was directly linked to the promotion of the environmentally sustainable use of the coast and also for the management of the Bay to be orientated towards its entirety rather than being limited to administrative boundaries. The initial response to the strategy led to the creation of a group incorporating all local authorities from around the Bay, together with English Nature, which identified two main tasks (Morecambe Bay Partnerships, 1996) as to:

- identify the important features and uses of the Bay; and

- suggest mechanisms and propose guidelines that would guide present and future activities.

The development of the Strategy was a gradual process and involved the local participation of over 1,000 people and organisations. Between 1993 and 1994, the emphasis lay in gathering information of the Bay and of the concerns of local people using a combination of questionnaires and local meetings. During 1995, the work was focussed upon identifying solutions to the issues raised by the local organisations and people. This led to the development of a series of working groups, in which over 120 individuals and organisations were actively involved. The findings of the working groups essentially guided the preparation of the Strategy.

The fundamental role of the Morecambe Bay Strategy is that of a tool for solving problems and, furthermore, it is important to recognise that it was evolved through the active participation of local organisations and individuals. However, it is not a statutory policy document and its implementation will only succeed if the proposals arising from it are both popular and practical. All interests must work together in a partnership, which must be based upon a clearly defined management framework, in order to ensure that the sustainable development and integration of activities should generate benefits to all interests around the Bay. The management framework is to be based upon the Morecambe Bay Standing Conference illustrated in Figure 2.

While the Morecambe Bay Strategy defines a series of ideas for the future management of the Bay, it cannot be implemented in isolation but through a policy of interdisciplinary co-operation. The Strategy should work in the support of other initiatives and has established an integrated policy with the following groups or initiatives, including:

- Morecambe Bay Conservation Group, an open group that meets to discuss a wide range of issues relating to the bay;
- Local Environment Agency Plans (LEAPS) prepared by the Environment Agency to identify the issues associated with the water management of river catchment areas;
- Morecambe Bay Shoreline Management Plan (SMP) to address the issues of coastal and flood defence throughout the Bay;
- Land Use Plans prepared by local planning authorities to guide development activities within their areas;

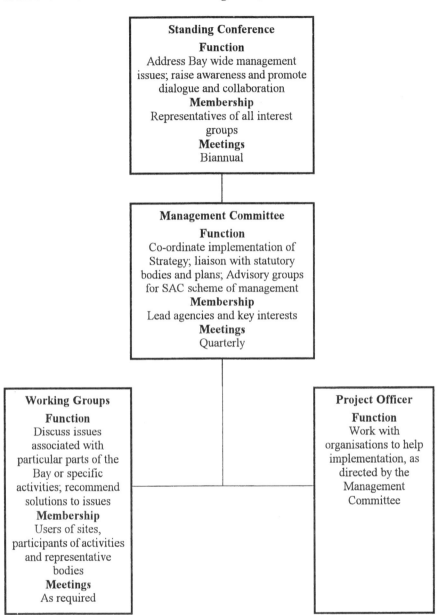

Figure 2 Management framework for implementing the Morecambe Bay Strategy

- Special Area of Conservation Scheme of Management as part of the EU habitats Directive.

The development of the Morecambe Bay Strategy is not an end in itself but part of an evolving process that will involve the local participation and interdisciplinary co-operation to ensure that the Bay is developed in a sustainable manner. The success of the Strategy will be dependent upon its flexibility and its ability to respond to new issues and developments. It will require frequent monitoring, auditing, consultation and review to ensure that the Strategy continues to play an important role in the integration of social, economic and environmental pressures.

Shoreline management plans (SMP)

The fundamental aim of the Shoreline Management Plan is the provision of a basis for sustainable coastal defence policies, which are defined by the Ministry of Agriculture, Fisheries and Food as ones which:

> take[s] account of the inter-relationships with other defences, developments and processes within a catchment or coastal cell or sub-cell and which avoid, as far as possible, tying future generations into inflexible and expensive options for defence (MAFF, 1995).

The fundamental objective of the SMP is to provide a strategy for an area that is both sustainable and furthermore permits the coast to be developed and used in the most sustainable manner, given its current use and state of development. This involves a considerable level of compromise and co-operation. Leafe *et al* (1998) considered that the two extremes varied between:

- the promotion of an unconstrained sustainable approach to coastal management as allowing the coastline to establish its natural position. This would, of course, result in abandonment of some dwellings and small settlements, the loss of farmland and some infrastructure; and
- the adoption of a policy to defend at all costs the land. This would result in existing defences having to be strengthened and new ones built to protect the land from the changing sea level.

In reality, a pragmatic approach is normally adopted that is somewhere between the two extremes. The SMP will play a key role in this issue by focussing the debate upon the choice between continuing to defend the coast at all costs or accommodating change without defence (Purnell, 1996). The major strength of the SMPs has been in setting up a dialogue on long-term coastal defence initiatives between adjacent coastal defence authorities. In this process, key issues have been identified, including a better understanding of coastal processes, which have led to some significant changes in direction in some areas (Hutchinson and Leafe, 1996). Leafe, *et al* (1998) consider that the most successful plans are characterised by:

- a well balanced team drawn from several disciplines (engineers, planners, geomorphologists, ecologists, archaeologists, etc.) and with extensive local knowledge;
- a flexible approach to the MAFF guidance document;
- a thorough consultation process (although great care is needed in the extent and timing of approaches made to the various interest groups);
- regular project meetings;
- a public consultation process;
- a political adoption process; and
- a well-planned and funded implementation process.

The original concepts of the SMP was initially investigated as a part of the Anglian Sea Defence Management Study, which provided a strategic assessment of the east coast of England between the Thames and the Humber (NRA, 1991). Research was subsequently undertaken to sub-divide the coast of England and Wales into a series of sediment cells and sub-cells, which essentially define the spatial limits for regional studies of coastal processes (HR, 1993). A total of 11 cells and 46 sub-cells were defined, the majority of these being used as the basis for the preparation of SMPs. Each SMP forms the basis for a non-statutory group of authorities responsible for the defence of the coast, thereby overcoming the constraints that were hitherto imposed by the administrative boundaries. The guidance provided by the MAFF (MAFF, 1995) recommends that the production of the SMP be divided into data collection and analysis, together with the setting of overall objectives, and the preparation of the plans. Within the first stage, it is specifically defined that the first step in setting up an SMP is to 'identify all those with an interest in the area' thereby emphasising the nature of inter-disciplinary co-operation. The nature of that co-operation will be described in specific detail when the Isle of Wight SMP is described below.

With regard to the future of SMPs and their ability to underpin sustainable development, they must begin to identify in both the medium and long term how we are to approach the way in which the coastal zone is to be used and defended. This will help formulate and plan what constraints those policies are likely to place upon coastal zone management in the future (Swash *et al*, 1995). This is a fundamental change in approach that will necessitate a research programme to ensure that the implementation of the plans is appropriate. Leafe *et al* (1998) suggested that the research will need to consider the following factors:

- how long-term adjustments (25-50 years) in land use can be developed within a planning system that currently works to a much shorter time-frame;
- how public participation and acceptance can be developed;
- how to measure and assess public perception and the demands for protection against the financial implications of not accommodating change in a sustainable manner at both local and national levels;
- more detailed feasibility studies to examine the management implementation options and economic implications of these options in more detail than has been possible in the current programme of SMPs;
- the scope for designing self-regulating protection schemes.

O'Riordan and Ward (1997) have explored the theory of legitimation and legitimacy in the context of participatory processes in SMPs. It was felt that local networks play an important role, especially when policy dilemmas such as strategic coastal retreat and the provision of land for coastal development occur. In many cases, an incipient network based upon co-operative individuals and organisations can be vital for sharing and disseminating information, and formulating positions.

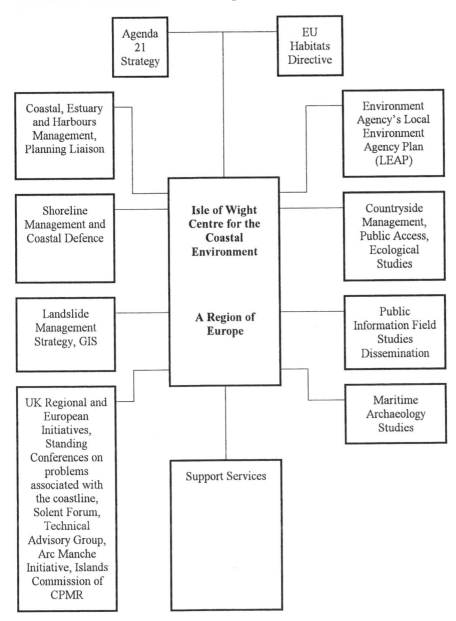

Figure 3 The key areas of activity for the Isle of Wight Centre for the Coastal Environment. *Source*: McInnes *et al*, 1998

The Isle of Wight SMP. The Isle of Wight has a very complex and varied geology. The geology is relatively soft and is very susceptible to coastal erosion. The wave direction is predominantly from the prevailing south-westerly direction. The conditions of the south coast are particularly unstable and wave attack has caused the largest urban landslide complex in north-west Europe (McInnes *et al*, 1998). An additional problem has been created as the result of favourable mico-climate experienced by the Isle of Wight, which has resulted over the last 150 years to more than 25% of the total coastline being subjected to intensive coastal urbanisation. Much of this is on the eastern coast. This provides a contrast to the western coast, which has been designated as a Heritage Coast. In addition, more than half of the island has been designated as an Area of Outstanding Natural Beauty and a large portion of the coast has been classified as a candidate site under Natura 2000. This has resulted in a relatively small island of approximately 250 km^2 being the intense subject of competing activities of development, recreation, tourism, industry, harbours, agriculture, fishing, mineral extraction and natural habitats, that all require consideration.

Since the mid-1980s there has been a growing awareness of coastal issues, particularly since two-thirds of the population (which is considerably enlarged during the summer months) live within 2 km of the coast. This eventually resulted in the publication, by the South Wight Borough Council of the *Management Strategy for the Coastal Zone* in 1993. This represented the first attempt to highlight the need for research and collaboration on coastal matters. Local government reorganisation in 1995 led to the replacement of the two former Borough Councils by a Unitary Authority, the Isle of Wight Council, which in turn has initiated work on a coastal zone management strategy for the entire coastline of the Isle of Wight (Jewell and Roberts, 1997). To a great extent, this work was overtaken by the introduction of SMPs, one of which consisted of the sub-cell of the Isle of Wight. McInnes *et al* (1998) identified the main objectives of this particular SMP as to:

- improve the level of understanding of the coastal process operating around the island;
- predict the likely future evolution of the coastline;
- identify all assets within the area covered by the SMP, which were likely to be affected by coastal change over the next 70 years;

- identify the need for regional and site specific research and investigations; and
- facilitate a process of consultation between those bodies with an interest in the shoreline.

The key areas of activity, which involves the SMP together with other initiatives such as UK regional and EU initiatives, are outlined in Figure 3.

In conclusion, the process of consultation and the implementation of the Isle of Wight SMP was made easier by the single tier system of local government and the recent coastal management strategies that had been undertaken prior to the introduction of the SMP. It was also aided by the high profile position of the island as a tourist resort and the active interest taken by the majority of islanders in coastal issues, given the relatively small size of the island, the effects of the sea, the proximity of the coast and the need to travel to the mainland. In terms of inter-disciplinary co-operation, the SMP process brought together such diverse professions as planning, civil engineering, ecology, and archaeology in the context of coastal defence, which strengthened the relationships between those disciplines and encouraged them to think in a more strategic manner about coastal issues.

Conclusion

The concept and context of sustainability is often confused and may be interpreted in a number of different ways. It is very easy to consider in a theoretical manner and when using abstract terms but when related to real situations, it is quite clear that sustainability can have different meanings depending upon ones perspective. This is especially so when viewed either from the position of coastal defence, as in the case of the settlement of Burling Gap, or from the environmentalist's perspective who strongly support the concept of natural processes and the full cycle of the sedimentary budget. Reality exists somewhere between the two extremes.

Despite the difficult nature of legislation within the coastal regions of England and Wales and the number of diverse bodies involved in the coastal regions, a surprising level of inter-disciplinary co-operation exists, mainly though the introduction of non-statutory programmes such as the Shoreline and Estuary Management Plans.

Throughout the coastal regions of England and Wales, there is indeed evidence of a high level of interdisciplinary co-operation towards the sustainable spatial development of the coastline of England and Wales. Many of the Forums, Strategies and Management Plans have adopted a pragmatic approach to sustainability, one which will not satisfy the demands from the two extremes, but one that will work in the majority of cases. It is, however, clear from the case studies that planning for development or even for conservation within the coastal and riparian regions must take into consideration far longer time scales than have previously been adopted.

References

Anon, 1996. Commissioner proposes measures to halt further decline in the EU's wetlands, *Natura,* **1**, 8-9, http://europa.eu.int/en/comm/dg11/news/natura/nat1en.htm (07/04/98).

Berkes, F. (ed.) 1989. *Common Property Resources: Ecology and Community-Based Sustainable Development,* Belhaven, London.

Blowers, A., 1992. Environmental policy: a quest for sustainable development, *Urban Studies,* **30**(4/5), 775-795.

Blowers, A., 1993. The time for change. In: Blowers, A. (ed.), *Planning for a Sustainable Environment,* Earthscan, London.

Bowers, J., 1997. *Sustainability and Environmental Economics, an Alternative Text,* Addison Wesley Longman Ltd., Harlow.

Council of the European Communities, 1995. *Progress Report on the Implementation of the European Community Programme of Policy and Action in Relation to the Environment and Sustainable Development Towards Sustainability,* COM(95) 624 Final., Strasbourg.

Council of the European Communities, 1996. *Demonstration Programme on Integrated Management of Coastal Zones,* European Commission Services, Information Document XI/79/96.

Council of the European Communities, 2000a. *Proposal for a European Parliament and Council Recommendation concerning the Implementation on Integrated Coastal Zone Management in Europe,* COM(2000) 545 final, 2000/0227 (COD), Brussels, 08/08/2000.

Council of the European Communities, 2000b. *Communication from the Commission to the Council and the European Parliament on Integrated Coastal Zone Management: a Strategy for Europe,* COM(2000) 547 final, Brussels, 27/09/2000.

Counsell, D., 1998. Sustainable development and structure plans in England and Wales: a review of current practice, *Journal of Environmental Planning and*

Management, **41**(2), 177-194.

Counsell, D., 1999. Sustainable development and structure plans in England and Wales: operationalizing the theories and principles, *Journal of Environmental Planning and Management,* **42**(1), 45-61.

Cullingworth, J.B. & Nadin, V., 1997. *Town and Country Planning in the UK (12th Ed.)*, Routledge, London.

Davidson, M., 1998. In peril from the sea, *The Daily Telegraph, Property Section,* 17, 15th August, London.

Davos, C.A., 1998. Sustaining co-operation for coastal sustainability, *Journal of Environmental Management,* **52**, 379-387.

Department of the Environment, 1992. *Policy Planning Guidance Note 20: Coastal Planning,* HMSO, London.

Department of the Environment, 1994. *Biodiversity Country Studies: Strategies and Action Plans for the UK,* Department of the Environment, London.

Dixon-Gough, R.W., 1999. The railway town: a case study in sustainable urban development. In: Dixon-Gough, R.W. (ed.), *Land Reform and Sustainable Development,* 251-265, Ashgate Publishing Ltd., Aldershot.

Dixon-Gough, R.W., 2001a. Partnerships in European coastal zone management. In: Dixon-Gough, R.W. (ed.), *European Coastal Zone Management,* 1-17, Ashgate Publishing Ltd., Aldershot.

Dixon-Gough, R.W., 2001b. Regional and international conflicts within the coastal zone. A case for partnerships and European-wide co-operation. In: Dixon-Gough, R.W. (ed.), *European Coastal Zone Management,* 1-17, Ashgate Publishing Ltd., Aldershot.

Doody, J.P., Pamplin, C.F., Gilbert, C. & Bridge, L., 1998. *Information Requirement for Integrated Coastal Zone Management,* Thematic Study F, European Union Demonstration Programme on Integrated Management in Coastal Zones, Study Contract Reference No.: 3050/STU/9700186.

Elliott, J.A., 1993. *An Introduction to Sustainable Development,* Chapman and Hall, London.

Environment Committee, 1992. *Coastal Zone Protection and Planning,* HMSO, London.

French, P.W., 1997. *Coastal and Estuarine Management,* Routledge, London.

Garner, R., 1996. *Environmental Politics,* Routledge, London.

Gibson, J., 1999. *Legal and Regulatory Bodies: Appropriateness to Integrated Coastal Zone Management,* Final Report to the European Commission - DG XI.D.2, Contract No.: B5-9500/97/000597/MAR/D2, MaCalister Elliott and Partners Ltd., Lymington, Hampshire, UK.

Hales, R., 2000. Land use planning and the notion of sustainable development: exploring constraint and facilitation within the English planning system, *Journal of Environmental Planning and Management,* **43**(1), 99-121.

Home, R., 2001. Raising the profile: River estuary management of the Lower Thames, Presented Paper at the *Second International Land Management Conference,* held at Anglia Polytechnic University, Chelmsford, England.

Humphrey, S. & Burbridge, P., 1999. *Planning and Management Processes: Sectoral and Territorial Co-operation,* Thematic Study D, European Demonstration Programme on Integrated Coastal Zone Management, Contract No.: ERDF 98.00.27.060, Department of Marine Science and Coastal Management, University of Newcastle.

Hutchinson, J. & Leafe, R.N., 1996. Shoreline Management Plans: a view to the way ahead. In: Fleming, C.A., *Coastal Management: Putting Policy into Practice.* Institute of Civil Engineers Conference Proceedings, Thomas Telford House, London.

Hydraulics Research, 1993. *Coastal Management: Mapping of Littoral Cells,* Hydraulics Research Report SR 328, Hydraulics Research, Wallingford.

IEEP, 1999. *The Influence of EU Policies on the Evolution of Coastal Zones,* Final Report of Thematic Study E, Study Contract ERDF No. 98.00.27.049, ICZM Demonstration Programme, Institute of European Environmental Policy, London.

Jewell, S. & Roberts, H., 1997. *Isle of Wight LIFE Project - Integrated Management of Coastal Zones,* Information Leaflet, Isle of Wight Council, Newport.

King, G., 1999. *Participation in the ICZM Processes: Mechanisms and Procedures Needed,* EC Demonstration Programme on ICZM, Final Report, NE80194, Hyder Consulting.

Kirklees Metropolitan District Council, 1989. *Kirklees State of the Environment Report.*

Leafe, R.N., Pethick, J. & Townend, I., 1998. Realising the benefits of shoreline management, *The Geographical Journal,* **164**(3), 282-290.

Local Government Management Board (LGMB), 1994. Community participation in local Agenda 21. In: *Local Agenda 21 Roundtable Guidance.*

Lusser, H., 1993. Environmental planning. In: Agyeman, J. & Evans, B. (eds.), *Local Environmental Policies and Strategies,* Longman, Harlow.

MAFF, 1995. *Shoreline Management Plans: a Guide for Coastal Defence Authorities,* Publication PB 2197, Ministry of Agriculture, Fisheries and Food and The Welsh Office, Association of District Councils, English Nature, National Rivers Authority, London.

McInnes, R.G., Jewell, S. & Roberts, H., 1998. Coastal management on the Isle of Wight, *The Geographical Journal,* **164**, 291-306.

McManus, P., 1996. Contested terrains: politics and discourses of sustainability, *Environmental Politics,* **5**(1), 48-73, 48-73.

Mitlin, D. & Satterthwaite, D., 1996. Sustainable development and cities. In: Pugh, C. (ed.), *Sustainability, the Environment and Urbanisation,* Earthscan, London.

Morecambe Bay Partnerships, 1996. *Morecambe Bay Strategy,* Morecambe Bay Partnerships, Grange-over-Sands.

National Rivers Authority, 1991. *The Future of Shoreline Management,* NRA Anglian Regional Conference Paper, Sir William Halcrow and Partners, Swindon.

O'Riordan, T., 1983. Putting trust in the countryside. In: *A Conservation and Development Programme in the UK,* 171-260, Kogan Page, London.

O'Riordan, T. & Ward, R., 1997. Building trust in shoreline management, *Land Use Policy,* **14,** 257-278.

Organisation for Economic Co-operation and Development, 1993. *Coastal Zone Management: Integrated Policies,* OECD, Paris.

Pethick, J., 1996. The sustainable use of coasts: monitoring, modelling and management. In: Jones, P.S., Healy, M.G. & Williams, A.T. (eds.), *Studies in European Coastal Management,* Samara Publishing Ltd., Cardigan.

Purnell, R.G., 1996. Shoreline Management Plans - national objectives and implementation. In: Fleming, C.A., *Coastal Management: Putting Policy into Practice.* Institute of Civil Engineers Conference Proceedings, Thomas Telford House, London.

Scott, A.J., 1996. The role of Coastal Forums in coastal zone management: case study of Cardigan Bay. In: Taussik, J. & Mitchell, J. (eds.), *Partnership in Coastal Zone Management,* Samara Publishing Ltd., Cardigan.

Scott, A.J., 1997. The role of forums in sustainable development: a case study of the Cardigan Bay Forum, *Journal of Sustainable Development,* **5,** 131-137.

Scott, A.J., 1998. The contribution of forums to rural sustainable development: a preliminary evaluation, *Journal of Environmental Management,* **54,** 291-303.

Seabright, P., 1993. Managing local commons: theoretical issues in incentive designs, *Journal of Economic Perspectives,* **7,** 113-119.

Selman, P., 1992. *Environmental Planning: The Conservation and Development of Biophysical Resources,* Paul Chapman Publishing, London.

Swash, A.R.H., Leafe, R.N. & Radley, G.P., 1995. Shoreline Management Plans and environmental considerations. In: Healey, M.G. & Doody, P. (eds.). *Directions in European Coastal Zone Management,* 161-167, Samara Publishing Ltd., Cardigan.

Taussick, J., 1997. Institutional frameworks in sustainable development: the example of coastal management, *International Sustainable Development Research Conference,* ERP, West Yorkshire.

Torgerson, D., 1995. The uncertain quest for sustainability: public discourse and the policies of environmentalism. In: Fisher, F. & Black, M. (eds.), *Greening of Environmental Policy,* Paul Chapman, London.

Turner, R.K. (ed.), 1988. *Sustainable Environmental Management: Principles and Practice,* Belhaven, London.

Turner, R.K., Lorenzoni, I., Beaumont, N., Bateman, I.J., Langford, I.H. & McDonald, A.L., 1998. Coastal Management for sustainable development.

analysing environmental and socio-economic changes on the UK coast, *Geographical Journal,* **164**(3), 269-281.

United Nations Conference on Environment and Development (UNCED), 1992. *Agenda 21: Programme of Action for Sustainable Development,* United Nations Department of Public Information, New York, USA.

Welsh Office, 1996. *A Working Countryside for Wales,* HMSO, Cardiff.

Weston, J. (ed.), 1997. *Planning and Environmental Impact Assessment in Practice,* Addison Wesley and Longman, Harlow.

Wilson, E., 1998. Planning and environmentalism in the 1990s. In: Allminder, P. & Thomas, H. (eds.), *Urban Planning and the British New Right,* Routledge, London.

World Coast Conference, 1993. *Preparing to Meet the Coastal Challenges of the 21st Stake-Holder Century,* Conference Report, Ministry of Transport, Public Works and Water Management, National Institute for Coastal and Marine Management /RIKZ, Coastal Zone Management Centre, The Netherlands.

World Commission on Environment and Development, 1987. *Our Common Future,* Oxford University Press, Oxford.

Managing the land under cloves and coconuts: the Zanzibar experience

Muhammad SULAIMAN
Ministry of Water, Construction, Energy, Lands and Environment, Zanzibar
Ali MIRZA, Shaibu JUMA and Veikko KORHONEN
Commission for Lands and Environment, Zanzibar

Abstract

As in many developing nations, land in Zanzibar remains the basic resource for all development activities and social needs. Viewed from this perspective, the fundamental challenge facing the government has been to ensure proper control of its use and exploitation. Introduction of a proper land administration system in the islands has always been at the centre of government plans and policies on effective land management.

Zanzibar has, over the decades, made tremendous effort to put the land administration system into order. Since the beginning of this century, the land administration machinery in the islands has been undergoing continuous changes in its structure, location, and mandate. Several institutional and legal reforms were introduced during the colonial era in an attempt to bring economic progress through efficient utilisation and control of the land resource. The 1964 revolution introduced radical land reform measures with diverse social and economic implications. The results of most of these changes have not been very encouraging in terms of bringing the anticipated economic and social development. Lack of success from these changes and the deteriorating economic situation over the recent years have forced the government to look for new economic policies that would promote serious investment programmes while ensuring sustainable exploitation of the land resource.

This paper reviews the struggle that has been going on over the years both during the colonial period and the post-revolutionary era. It specifically highlights the achievements of these efforts, the current activities and plans, and provides a glimpse of the way ahead.

Land administration - the colonial era

Two systems of land holding existed in Zanzibar before 1964. There were private and government land holding patterns. These patterns lasted up to 1964 when all land was vested in the government for the benefit of the public. Communal land holding continued to exist as the government allowed people to exercise their communal rights. However, land disputes were common due to mainly unsurveyed property boundaries. The boundaries were normally marked by the use of permanent trees such as mango trees, coconut trees, clove trees, and the like, as well as the use of semi-permanent trees like 'mibono' and 'mifurusadi'.

Due to land disputes, which were increasing at an alarming rate, the government decided to intervene. In 1934, Sir Ernest Dowson, was called upon to give some advisory ideas on measures to curb the situation. He suggested that there was a need to have clear permanent boundaries in each defined administrative area, commonly referred to as 'Shehia', by the use of cadastral blocks. These shehias were to be surveyed with the aid of aerial photography. The photographs could then be used for supporting a land registry. His suggestions were later tried out. The government accepted Sir Ernest's ideas and a new Bill for Settlement and Registration of Rights on land was prepared in 1937.

However, the work could not be easily done at first because big tracts of land had been mortgaged to individuals who had yet to recover their money. This became a setback to the government plan for it became necessary for the government to pay all debtors first so as to regain the land in its control. In 1938, the Land Protection (Debt settlement) Decree was introduced to serve the purpose. This Law was applied hand-in-hand with the Land Alienation Decree of 1934, which had been introduced to safeguard the right of individuals on matters related to land ownership.

Systematic land surveying came to an end in the years 1939-1945, during the Second World War, and hence the Survey Department became part of the Public Works Department (PWD) in 1946. In 1958, the government invited Mr Les Howells to assist in the formation of a new department on matters attached to surveying and ownership of land in the country. Mr Howells prepared a report on the 'Possibilities of Cadastral Survey with an Accompanying Settlement of Rights to Land within the Zanzibar Protectorate'. This report suggested an attempt to survey the land countrywide. Nevertheless, the move could not be applied due to the high cost involved. In spite of the fact that there was an Administrator General, there was no guarantee of title to land in the country. Land parcels and ownership were registered under the Registration of Documents Decree of 1919, Land under the Wakf fell under the Commission for Wakf according to the Wakf Property Decree and later on under the Wakf and Trust Property Decree of 1967 and 1980.

Post-revolutionary land reforms

The whole set up of land administration changed completely after the 1964 Revolution. Three laws emerged, which governed land ownership and distribution. The first law was Decree No 13 of 1965. This Decree vested all land in the State. This law became effective from 8th March. 1964. The second law was the Confiscation of Immovable Property Decree, i.e. Decree No 8 of 1964 and the last was the Land Distribution Decree, Decree No 5 of 1966 which was later amended by Decree No 10 of 1969. All these decrees empowered the President to own all land on behalf of the government and to distribute it to the public. Three-acre plots in the rural areas and residential plots in the urban areas were all distributed in accordance with the above decrees. The distribution of three-acre plots was based on the following aspects:

- that the plot could not be inherited through the inheritance provisions;
- that it was not allowed to be sold, sub-divided or otherwise used contrary to the purpose intended;
- that the plot could not be leased or mortgaged.

The expiring of the right of occupancy is something new to the indigenous people of Zanzibar. The system of giving strict terms of occupation to landholders has therefore caused the majority of the people to be wary to develop land to the required standard. Although there has not been a case where a right has been terminated, the slow rate of land development by individuals has called for the government to restructure the whole system of land ownership in the country. Among the problems which existed in the past is the absence of an effective approach to the management and administration of land resources by different organs responsible for such duties. As a result, the government found it necessary to have effective land management and administrative procedures. In 1982, the first proposals on land policy were presented.

The government accepted the proposals in 1985. Along with these proposals, in 1985 the Ministry of Water, Construction and Energy Resources through Overseas Development Administration (ODA) of the United Kingdom managed to work together with Mr J.C.D. Lawrance who reviewed the possibility of introducing land registration in the country. In his report on land tenure and his preparation of the draft legislation for establishing a system of land registration in Zanzibar, Mr Lawrance suggested that there should be a law, which would recognise the person responsible for holding and developing a particular piece of land, in hand with land surveying and registration laws.

Recent changes in land policy

Following the report by Mr Lawrance on land policy, a special land use committee was formed in 1988. The Committee intended to propose the best approach to be followed for effective land administration to the government. Among other things, the Committee proposed the necessity of introducing a single organ that would he responsible for issues related to land and management of the environment, rather than many organs, which performed similar and related functions.

In 1989, the government formed the Commission for Lands and Environment (COLE). The formation of COLE has enabled all matters concerning land management along with land use to be dealt with under one umbrella. Within this Commission, there are three departments. These are the Department of Lands, the Department of Survey and Urban Planning, and the Department of Environment. Currently, the Commission For Lands and Environment is under the Ministry of Water, Construction, Energy, Lands and Environment.

Recent legal reforms

Following various studies and recommendations, the Government of Zanzibar has recently passed different legislation that forms part of the overall programme to regularise the land holding arrangements on the two islands.

The initial effort produced the Land Adjudication Act, the Registered Land Act, and the Land Survey Act, which were passed in 1989. More recently, the Land Tenure Act, the Land Transfer Act and the Land Tribunal Act have been enacted. This legislation provides the basic legal framework, which is a prerequisite for the implementation of positive land reforms, the organising and maintenance of the cadastre, the improvement of land administration practices and general land information management.

A review of the key elements of these Acts should provide a clear indication of the commitment and the course, which Zanzibar is determined to take.

The Land Adjudication Act

The Land Adjudication Act lays down the procedures for carrying out the process of determining rights and interests to land. These include: the declaration of certain areas as adjudication areas; the appointment and definition of powers of special officers and committees; the collection and processing of claims and evidence, preparation and presentation of adjudication records and hearing disputes and appeals.

Under the Land Adjudication Act, the islands will be divided first into adjudication areas and then into sections to systematically bring all the properties into the process, in manageable units. An adjudication area is declared by public notice in the Gazette and any person claiming an interest to land within the relevant Section shall make his claim in the manner and within the period fixed by the relevant notice. Following that claim period, the Demarcation, Surveying, and Recording Officers will commence the work of determining the rights and extent of every piece of land within that section.

Immediately after the adjudication process is over, the plots will be surveyed and a cadastral map produced together with the adjudication record with respect to every parcel of land in that area. A notice will be issued of the completion of the record and of the place at which the record can be inspected together with the map. Objections against the adjudication record can he raised and heard by the adjudication officer who shall notify all persons to be affected and determine the claim.

When all the claims have been settled and the adjudication record finalised, the final record will be submitted to the Registrar together with all the documents retained after adjudication. The Registrar will prepare a registry map and a land register for the whole area out of the final adjudication record and the cadastral map. Appeals to the Land Tribunal against the final adjudication record are allowed and also to the appellate court where an issue of law is involved.

The Registered Land Act

The Act provides for the systematic (compulsory) compilation of the land register throughout the islands of Zanzibar. Under the Registered Land Act, the exercise will be carried out on an area by area basis, each area forming a registration district. This approach has been found to be more appropriate in compiling a land register that will support the development of a multi-purpose cadastre and, ultimately, the introduction of a modern land information system to the isles. The Land Register will contain three sections:

- *the property section* containing a brief description of the land or lease together with particulars of its appurtenances and reference to the registry map, if any;
- *the proprietorship section* showing particulars of the proprietor of the land or lease and any restrictive covenants affecting his right of disposition or use;
- *the encumbrances section* containing particulars of every encumbrance and every right adversely affecting the land or lease.

The Act introduces a new concept of 'statutory trusts'. The purpose is to control multiple ownership, i.e. fragmentation of ownership (right to occupancy) as opposed to fragmentation of land. A statutory trust is created when more than ten persons are registered as 'proprietors in common'. Otherwise, all undivided shares in land would require registration and clutter the register. It will also make proper use and development of the land impossible. Families are given the option of appointing their own trustees and making their own decisions on how to deal with their land.

There is great emphasis on keeping the register up to date. Once the property has been registered, all subsequent dealings concerning that property must be reflected in the register to be valid. The register provides a governmental guarantee of all the interests registered. Except for certain overriding interests such as easements and profits, a registered proprietor secures indefeasible rights against any interests and claims whatsoever.

Any person dealing with a registered piece of land or lease does not have to investigate the circumstances and validity of previous transactions. One can safely rely on the information contained in the register. The Act provides that any person who suffers loss or damage through mistakes or omissions made in the register shall be entitled to receive indemnity.

There is, however, no guarantee on measurements and no compensation to anyone who is found to have contributed to the damage, omission, or mistake.

The Land Survey Act

The new Land Survey Act is a comprehensive piece of legislation which has been drafted to support the needs of a modern land registration system, i.e. the demand for an unambiguous definition of every parcel on the register, supported by a survey plan. It repeals the old Land Survey Decree (Cap 100) of 1911 which was too brief and incapable of providing proper guidance on the conduct of surveyors in the islands.

The Director of Surveys to be appointed under the Act will have the responsibility of supervising, directing and controlling all cadastral surveys in Zanzibar. He will also he responsible for the examination and approval of survey plans. Of particular importance in this Act is the official involvement of private surveyors in carrying out cadastral surveys in the islands. The Act provides for the establishment of a Land Surveyors' Board which will be responsible for granting licenses to practice land surveying in Zanzibar. The Board, which will be under the chairmanship of the Director of Surveys will take responsibility to ensure that the professional conduct of surveys is in accordance with the law and regulations.

The Land Tenure Act

The Land Tenure Act was designed to define all land relationships in Zanzibar. It replaces all the post-revolution decrees and goes considerably further than the previous Decrees in defining and setting out the manner in which the tenurial system is meant to operate. The underlying feature of the new Land Tenure Act is the retention of the concept that the absolute ownership of all land in the islands of Zanzibar is vested in the Government. All land is therefore referred to as public land. However, a freehold styled system of private holding is developed at a secondary level which goes beyond a traditional leasehold title, but does not go as far as ownership.

People are entitled to hold land through a 'right of occupancy' to be granted by the Government or on a leasehold basis. Right to occupancy is the highest legal status of possession, which can be claimed by a landholder. All Zanzibaris are entitled to right of occupancy, which can be obtained through government grants, inheritance, purchase, or gift.

Holders of a right to occupancy enjoy practically the same rights one would otherwise obtain in a freehold system and for all intents and purposes the interests have the same meaning as ownership.

Grants of public land are an integral part of the land tenure system. Each Zanzibari of eighteen years or over is entitled to receive one government grant of agricultural land and two of urban land during his/her lifetime. Grants of land for commercial or industrial purposes can be made without any limitations as long as the proposal for the land use is not in conflict with the National Land Use Plan.

Grants shall be made on a provisional basis of three years during which period an individual will be evaluated to determine if he should receive a permanent order of grant. During this period, land can not be transferred. The Act sets maximum and minimum limitations regarding the size of agricultural plots. Grants of agricultural land are limited to a maximum of eight hectares. Individual parcels with an area of less than 0.6ha will not be acceptable. The maximum allotment does not apply to communal holdings and in a situation where land is not acquired by government grant.

To control fragmentation, no individual parcels of land may be sub-divided into an area of less than 0.6 ha. In a case where such a situation would occur, the land shall be held jointly.

The Government can lease public land, which is not comprised in a right of occupancy. All leases shall be inheritable and renewable. Initially, government leases shall be granted for a maximum of forty-nine years. No lease can be sold or sub-leased. Any proprietor can lease his right of occupancy or part of it as long as the leasehold period does not exceed fifteen years.

A reasonable service charge will be imposed on both urban and agricultural lands based on the use and value of the land. This is expected to discourage individuals from leaving their land idle and land speculators, as they will have to pay charges for land which they do not use.

114

There are provisions for terminating a right of occupancy if the Government declares that there is an abiding issue of national interest involved. But, in order to terminate any right for this reason, there must be a hearing before the Land Tribunal during which the Government ought to present clear and convincing evidence to warrant the repossession. The market value must also be paid for the land and any unexhausted improvements prior to the issuance of an order of termination. To ensure the proper use of land resources the Government shall have the right to repossess any 'abandoned' or 'idle' land after giving sufficient time and warning to the proprietor.

The Land Transfer Act

The Land Transfer Act is basically a supplement of the Land Tenure Act. It provides a mechanism for scrutinising the permanent transfer of long-term leases or land from a private landholder. It creates special procedures which ensure that only *bona fide* transfers can he registered and that the process does not give rise to a transaction that does not conform to the Land Tenure Act, the Registered Land Act or any other relevant Act. At the same time, the Act has been designed to protect indigenous land-holders from being swindled out of their land by unscrupulous land developers and speculators. There are restrictions that control any dealing that will be seen as not in the best interests of the transferor or which may potentially threaten the welfare of his own family.

The Act provides for the composition of a special committee to be known as the Land Transfer Committee which will be responsible for reviewing and approving all requests for a long term transfer of a right to occupancy or long term lease interests. Any land holder who intends to transfer his interest through the sale, lease, gift or any valuable consideration must submit a special application to the Land Transfer Committee specifying the reasons behind the transfer.

Under the Land Transfer Act, all leases of more than ten years are considered to be long term leases and fall under the provisions of this Act. Interests to he transferred through transmission by inheritance are not subject to the procedures under the Land Transfer Act. The various reasons where the Committee may withhold consent for a transfer of land or long term lease are stipulated in the Act. These include situations when the Committee is of the opinion that the permanent transfer or lease of such land would deprive the transferor or lessor of needed resources to support his family. Likewise, where the Committee feels that the use of the land would be inappropriately changed, or where the provisions of the Registered Land Act or any other relevant Act are violated. Any applicant whose request for a land transfer has been rejected by the Committee is entitled to appeal to the Land Tribunal.

The Land Tribunal Act

The Land Tribunal Act is considered a vital piece of legislation that had to be in place before the start of the comprehensive land rationalisation program in the islands. The envisaged land adjudication, land demarcation, registration and land consolidation programmes arc likely to be accompanied by a variety of disputes concerning boundaries, ownership and other land issues.

   The various land reform measures over the years, policy changes and a general lack of proper documents concerning land and properties may all provoke considerable land cases in the cause of implementing the land rationalisation programme.

   The Land Tribunal Act provides for the creation of an informal court to be known as the Land Tribunal that will deal with land matters. This is a special court, which will sit separately on both islands with a wide jurisdiction over land issues. The Tribunal is set to deal with a broad range of disputes concerning land but does not prevent formal courts from hearing any land matter that involves an issue of law. It will still be possible for such matters to be heard by an appropriate appellate court as a matter of judicial review.

   The Chairman of the Tribunal shall he a senior magistrate with the appropriate legal training. Disputes on issues such as the location of a property boundary, misuse of land or whether further subdivision of a certain piece of land should he allowed or otherwise shall he heard by the Land Tribunal. Also included are issues relating to any distribution of land which will take place, any complaint arising out of an adjudication process and all issues involving any claims that proprietors might make that should be processed through a court. The Act explicitly includes all issues relating to registration.

Developments in surveying and mapping

The geodetic network

The most recent triangulation measurement in Zanzibar was by the Directorate of Overseas Surveys in 1977. The network was established to provide control points for the topographical mapping of Zanzibar at a scale of 1:10,000 using aerial photography. At that time the only possible way of getting observations for a triangulation network in a terrain like Zanzibar's, was by using observation towers and tall structures like water towers and lighthouses as observation points. Some of the triangulation points were actually located on these features. Later on, when the structures do become obsolete, those points are difficult to reuse. Another problem in Zanzibar has been the erosion of shoreline corals. Many of the old points were constructed quite close to the shoreline on top of coral cliffs and due to erosion many of them have fallen into the sea over the last fifteen years. The methods used in 1977 were theodolite observations and tellurometer measurements.

Owing to the above reasons a new basic network measurement was considered to be necessary to form a homogenous density of control points for any future measurements for both Unguja and Peniba islands. The approach was to measure twin points that were visible to each other, to facilitate orientation in any later measurements. The points are located not far from roads so that they are easy to reach. The rough distribution of twin points in Unguja, where the vegetation and topography are easier, is one twin point within every four kilometres along the roads and in Pemha, every three kilometres. The network has a total number of 610 points: one twin point, every 12 km^2 in Unguja and every 6 km^2 in Pemha.

The measurements took only eight weeks in January-February 1992. Nine GPS receivers, manufactured by Ashtech Inc., were used. Six of the receivers were two-channel models and three, older, one-channel models. The observation windows allowed three minimum 1.5 hour sessions daily. The first order measurements, including the connection measurements between both islands, were observed in long overnight sessions.

Different adjustment variations were tested especially to test the accuracy of the old triangulation network. Finally it was decided to only use the minimum amount of points as fixed horizontal controls: the Obs Spot point in Zanzibar town and the Chake Chake water tower point. These two points were also used when the connection to the mainland triangulation network was established in 1977, using a combination of tellurometer and JMR-doppler system observations. Without the knowledge of the local geoid, and because of the lack of a first order levelling network (the biggest problem being in Pemba), the adjustment of heights could not be absolutely correct. There is still an urgent need to do a comprehensive first order levelling including long term sea level observations and the direction of gravity observations on both islands.

Surveying and mapping techniques

When considering the accuracy suitable for measuring boundaries, keeping in mind that the total amount of boundary corner points will be around 700,000 pieces, an estimated target accuracy of ± lm in rural areas and ± 10 cm in town areas has been decided upon.

By using the Global Positioning System (GPS) points as reference points, it is always possible to do surveying using the traditional traverse and polar tachymeter measurement system. Traverse networks have been measured on the two pilot adjudication areas, keeping in mind the further mapping of boundaries and also testing the twin point system. Portable, light GPS equipment has also been considered as a tool for the surveying of the boundaries and tests will be done during the pilot phase of the suitability and accuracy of the instruments. In the case of using GPS measurements, the basic network is used for reference points. The third method, which will be tested, is to measure bearings with accurate hand compasses and distances with a tape. In the latest test, the measurements will be adjusted using blocks surrounded by traverses and a triangulation network adjustment program. In town areas, the old co-ordinates will be used where they are reliable.

In Zanzibar, both agricultural and dwelling parcels are small and it means that the cadastral map scale must be quite large. This means that a huge number of map sheets need to be kept updated if a traditional cadastral map system is used. Another approach is to have the map updating computerised, initially only plotting a series of maps and producing partial map sheets only when changes have taken place.

The boundary map is a numerical element showing control points, boundary lines, and corner points, together with their numbers and parcel numbers. Another element will be the base map. Different variations are being and will continue to be tested to find the most suitable base map, such as line maps, aerial photo enlargements and scanned aerial photos. A digital orthophoto will also be tested, which will be done using existing aerial photography at a scale of 1:25,000.

In towns (Zanzibar town in Unguja and Wete, Chake Chake and Mkoani towns in Pemba) there are existing line maps, which will be used as base maps. The scales will vary from 1:500 in Zanzibar Stone Town to 1:10,000 in coral rag areas where there are no permanent private parcels but large communal holdings.

The adjudication trials

The adjudication process is the most critical task of the entire land registration exercise. Effective and experienced adjudicators can only overcome the natural resistance and misunderstandings of land claimants and other potential landholders. The lack of suitably trained personnel has initially been the most serious obstacle to get the adjudication running smoothly. The operational procedures and rules of adjudication are precisely defined in the Land Adjudication Act of 1989. They are being followed as set out. Before commencement of the field operation in the adjudication area, the Minister appointed the Adjudication Officer for the area. The Adjudication Officer in turn appointed the Demarcation, Recording, and Survey Officers. The plan for the adjudication during this project phase was that the Minister would appoint two Adjudication Officers: one for Unguja and one for Pemba. The pilot work in Unguja has started.

The first phase has been to mount a publicity campaign to explain what is happening to the landowners, what the project teams will do and what the land holders (claimants) must do. This has involved the use of radio broadcasts, newspaper notices, video/TV programmes, about adjudication and registration, and a series of public meetings. Naturally, all local officials were fully briefed before any local meetings took place. The adjudication pilot area in Unguja is located approximately ten miles from Zanzibar town. To make access to the adjudication office easier for the landholders and also to get the field work co-ordination closer to the activities, an adjudication field office has been established inside the area.

The area has been divided into sections, and claimants for each section have been called to make their claims at the declared time period. Claimants who have legal or other documentary evidence are required to submit their documents, which are copied for the claim file and stamped to prevent people reusing them. Claimants who have no documents to support their claim are encouraged to submit a properly notarised affidavit, which contains the relevant information about the details required.

The claimants have been requested, together with all neighbours, to show and clear their boundaries and assist in planting the beacons. During this phase the Demarcation Officer produces a demarcation form which is included in the claim file.

During the process of receiving claims and of demarcation, some disputes have occurred. There have been ownership disputes when some lessees have claimed ownership but most have been boundary disputes where neighbours do not agree on the location of their boundaries. In most cases, the Demarcation Officers and in some cases the Adjudication Officer has been able to solve the dispute.

Consolidation of irrigated rice lands

In the early 1970s the Government made a decision that the lands of four irrigated areas would be designated for rice production, one of the staples of the Zanzibar diet. It was to be the initial attempt to make the Isles self-sufficient in rice. To do this there were allocations made of 0.10 ha for the production of rice. It was determined that this would provide as many people as possible with the opportunity to produce the rice that was so important to their diet. Unfortunately, these allocations did not create a system in which there was self-sufficiency. Virtually all of the country's rice was still imported and an estimate was made that, even when productivity was high, a typical family did not produce more than their needs for one month per annum. Even those few people who had multiple allocations (n * 0.10 ha), did not meet the annual needs of a family. At the same time, many farmers did not assume their responsibilities for maintaining the canals on which their parcels were located. A system of Farmers Associations was established. However, the administration of the Associations proved to be extremely difficult. Many individuals and their immediate family members or other close relatives had more than one allocation located in areas administered by different Associations.

With this background, it was felt that a proper allocation of the rice lands should be made. First of all, each parcel should be a minimum, of 0.50 ha in order to more effectively meet the defined needs. Secondly, it was imperative that each allottee be responsible to only one Farmers' Association. This would be a basic consideration in the re-allocations.

Finally, it was felt that an allocation scheme should be designed to attempt to improve the maintenance of the canals.

There was no problem in reallocating these lands as the holding of each person is always re-allotted at the beginning of each cropping season. If the land was allotted to the same person, growing season after growing season, it was felt that an attempt should be made to determine if there were grounds to allot the land to the farmer on a permanent basis, including rights of inheritance, etc. Therefore, as part of the ZILEM activities of the Commission for Lands and Environment, a co-ordinating group from the Commission and the Ministry of Agriculture, Livestock and Natural Resources was put together to determine if a consolidation was necessary. After the group determined there was a need, it was asked to oversee and assist in the development of a procedure. The first activity was to develop a process for determining a background analysis and secondly, to set out a data base through which the re-allocation procedures and the recipients of the parcels could be put in place.

Thus, the activities necessary for carrying out the consolidation began. An assessment to determine the qualitative character of each farmer's participation was made. This was done with the aim of assessing exactly who should be given the permanent allocation. A five-point scale for this assessment was developed. However, this scale was inadequate for a variety of reasons. It did not discriminate with precision among the farmers. Therefore, a second scale was developed and a further assessment took place among the farmers who scored in the top two categories of the initial five-point assessment. The second assessment had thirteen criteria, which were quite specific. They were set up to evaluate how the farmers assumed the responsibilities necessary for effective cultivation of irrigated rice in Zanzibar. This second assessment proved to be effective and set the stage for the development of the technical implementation of the consolidation programme.

As part of the assessment and the creation of the database, all related persons, who were willing to work co-operatively with their kin, were grouped together in 'family' groups. The idea was, where possible, to bring the families together on the same canal in order to enhance the likelihood that there would be co-operation in the distribution of water and maintenance of the canals. Membership in a family group by itself, however, did not ensure an allocation in the consolidation, as any individual farmer who scored below the cut-off point in the evaluation that applied to all farmers would not be eligible for a parcel in the irrigated zone at this time. Since the parcels were to be five times as large under the consolidation, it was clear that there would be fewer allottees. Thus, the allotment procedure had to be carried out with extreme care.

Firstly, the maps of all four irrigated rice schemes were digitised using MapInfo. Secondly, all the social data was entered in a separate data base (dBase IV). The two databases were then linked so that it became possible to determine:

- where each allottee had parcels;
- how the scheme would look if each allottee's multiple parcels were located together;
- how the reallocation scheme would look if the persons with the highest evaluation scores were each given individual allotments of 0.50 ha;
- how the allotment procedure would be carried out by putting families of three or more persons together on the same canal; and finally,
- to determine which configuration of individual and family parcels made more sense in creating a consolidated pattern of holdings that would satisfy, as closely as possible, all of the criteria of the co-ordinating group.

The process has now been developed so that the first real trials of reallocation are ready to take place in the Pilot Adjudication Area of the ZILEM project. The Mtwango Irrigated Rice Cultivation Scheme, covering an area of approximately 68 ha, will be consolidated by the time this paper is presented.

The planned land registration system

Preparations for the implementation of the national land registration programme are now in the final stages. The basic legal framework is already in place and plans are currently underway to chart out the implementation strategies. The results from the two pilot study areas shall provide the initial records for the compilation of the land registry.

The land register is to be kept open to the public. Any one interested shall be entitled to a certified copy of the register or any part of it. Once a parcel is registered, any subsequent dealings concerning such parcel must be reflected in the register for such dealing to be legally valid. In conjunction with the plan for compiling the manual land register, a prototype computerised land information system called 'ZALIS' has been developed. The approach has been to make the system as simple as possible concerning the computers and programs. The system has been created to run with PC level computers, the main computer being a Pentium with an optical disk drive. A digitiser and plotters are part of the system. Ultimately, all the Departments of the Commission for Lands and Environment will be connected to the system by a network, Land Register data being only a part of the whole database. Of course strict limitations in using and especially in updating different kinds of data will exist.

The main software used during the development of the systems are Windows (Word for Windows, Excel), Dbase IV, and MapInfo. For calculation of co-ordinates, a triangulation and traverse network adjustment program from the Finnish National Land Survey (MMH PC300) and a tachymeter data transfer, calculation and plotting program called Minimap have been used. It is estimated that there will be 10-20 transactions per day in the Land Registration Office. As each land transaction is registered, the information is recorded by hand on paper. The forms are then carried to the computer and a trained operator inputs the information. When required, the computer can print out reports on paper, which may go to the Land Registration Office, the public, or the Land Registration Archives. Data on the computer is stored on the hard disk, with backups and archiving done on optical disks.

The way ahead

The available legal framework and the present institutional structure all provide the ideal set up for the smooth implementation of the new land policies and programmes. However, the implementation of the various measures, which are planned for the realisation of the new land management policies, requires serious commitment and the availability of qualified personnel and reliable resources. Zanzibar faces formidable constraints in both these areas. There is a serious lack of local expertise, acute shortage of equipment and limited financial resources.

As previously stated, in a developing country one of the most serious problems is to find capable personnel of filling the main posts. Finding a Registrar of Lands and a Deputy for Pemba island has been a long search and it is still continuing. A special requirement for the candidate is that he should be able to develop himself in adopting modern data handling techniques, which will be used to make the first registration and the updating of the system effective. The initial cost of introducing the new system is well beyond the economic capability of the Zanzibar government. In this respect, continued donor funding is considered an essential element of the programme.

The climate, especially the hot, humid, dusty and salty air necessitates quite special demands for the archives and computer premises. As an example, in normal local conditions a fungus affects a floppy disk after an average of three months so that it is no longer usable. The stability of power voltages is poor and power cuts are very common, varying from a couple of hours to a couple of days. This emphasises the importance of careful planning from the very beginning. Planning should determine the essential requirements (including training), set priorities, and evaluate the viability of the different proposals. The current pilot projects should provide an opportunity for assessing the time, the cost, the techniques, and for determining the appropriate implementation strategies.

Whatever the case, implementation of the proposed land adjudication and registration programmes is a daunting task for Zanzibar. There is certainly a serious determination on the part of the government to take up the challenge. What is not so certain is the capability of the government to absorb the financial and social implications involved and, on the other hand, the continuation of the long-term support from donors.

References

Howells, L.J., 1960. *Report on the Possibilities of Cadastral Survey with an Accompanying Settlement of Rights to Land within the Zanzibar Protectorate*, Internal Report.

Lawrance, J.C.D., 1985. *Report by Land Tenure Advisor on Preparation of Draft Legislation for Establishing a System of Land Registration in Zanzibar*, Internal Report.

Saad Yahya & Associates, 1982. *Land Policy for Zanzibar and Pemba*, Internal Report.

The state and proposals for changes for rural land management in Poland

Andrzej HOPFER, Ryszard CYMERMAN and Andrzej NOWAK
Department of Regional Planning, University of Agriculture and Technology, Olsztyn, Poland

Abstract

Rural land in Poland covers about 80% of the country and creates very significant problems regarding its legal state, future function, use, and economical value. There are two main features, which strengthen reasons for carrying research and looking for results to help both the government and farmers in rural land management in Poland: the problems of restructuring the size, number and economical status of private farms, and the problems concerning the distribution or re-distribution of the rural land remnants of the former, State Land Fund and State Rural Farms, hold by the Agency of State Owned Rural Land.

The paper presents the current state of the matter, its analysis, proposals for the future, and alternating solutions. The period of the 1990s was a time of important transformations in physical management, not only in urban areas but also of active transformations in typically rural areas. This is mainly linked to the liquidation of the State owned farms, which caused problems in distribution and use of their former areas. This created conditions favourable for rationalisation in physical management and area restructuring of the private farms. Large-scale transformations in the ownership of rural real properties apply also, although to a lesser extent, to the use of rural areas.

The structure of usage for rural areas

The structure of usage of the rural land of the country is dominated by agricultural and forests. The status at the end of 1994 consisted of agricultural land (arable land, orchards, meadows, and pastures) occupying 59.6% of the land, and forests and wooded areas some 28.1% of the geographic area of the country. As a consequence, there was 0.48 ha of agricultural land and 0.23 ha of forests and wooded areas for every citizen of the country.

This structure differs significantly from province to province. The highest share of agricultural land is encountered in the provinces of Skierniewice (77.9%), Płock (77.1%), and Ciechanów (74.5%). The lowest percentage of agricultural land is found in provinces of Zielona Góra (39.9%), Gorzów (41.6%) and Krosno (42.4%). The largest percentage of forests is found in the provinces of Zamość (48.6%), Krosno (47.2%) and Gorzów (44.8%). Critically low percentages of forests are found in provinces of: Płock (11.9%), Skierniewice (13.7%), and Łódź (14.7%). By contrast, the nation-wide percentage share of area occupied by transport is 3.2%, settlements 3.2%, water bodies 2.7%, wasteland 1.6%, and mining 0.1%, is low.

The changes in the to the land use structure are of limited character. This results from the barriers imposed in the transfer of agricultural and forest land for purposes of urbanisation and investments that are stipulated in the provisions of the Act on Physical Development (1994) and the Act on the Protection of Agricultural and Forest Lands (1995). During the period between 1991-1994, 25,855 ha of land were taken from agricultural use across the nation (19.9% of which was Class I through Class III land). Of that area, 3,516 ha were used for afforestation and the planting of woodland (GUS, 1995). During that same period, 2,134 ha of forested land were taken from use (including 8.1% of land on the most fertile habitats, i.e. fresh, moist and marsh forest as well as mountain forest). The productivity of agricultural land assessed according to the percentage of respective fertility classes of soil in the area (at 1994) is illustrated in Table 1.

Table 1 The productivity of agricultural land

Separate Soil Classes						
I	II	III	IV	V	VI	(Viz)
0.4	2.9	22.3	39.8	22.7	11.9	(0.9)

The land occupied by classes V to VI, which is of low value for agricultural production, represents a third of the total agricultural land area. The natural reasons justify a change in the qualification of such land for either investment or afforestation purposes.

Ownership transformations after 1990

Individuals own the largest proportion of agricultural land in Poland and at the end of 1994, 80.3% was privately owned. This percentage, however, differs from province to province. The lowest percentage of privately owned agricultural land is in the provinces of Gorzów 48.4%, Zielona Góra 50.5%, and Koszalin 52.0%. The highest percentage of agricultural land owned by individuals is in the provinces of Ostrołęka 98.2%, Łomża 97.9%, and Sieradz 96.6%.

During the period between 1991-1994, an increase in the percentage of privately owned agricultural land rose by 5.5%. The largest changes towards the increase in the share of privately owned agricultural land have been recorded in those provinces that formerly had a large share of agricultural land owned by the State Treasury. Similarly, in the same period, the average area of agricultural land per individual farm increased from 6.6 ha to 7.4 ha. The major phenomenon behind this increase in the area of the farms was the purchase of land from the Agricultural Property Resources of the State Treasury. The percentage change in the area of agricultural land used by different size groups of farms is illustrated in Table 2.

Table 2 The percentage change in the area of agricultural land holdings

Year	Division of the agricultural land into farm size groups (in ha)								
	1-2	2-5	5-7	7-10	10-15	15-20	20-30	30-50	over 50
1991	17.6	35.3	14.9	14.8	11.3		6.1		
1994	21.7	32.8	13.3	13.4	11.0	4.4	2.4	0.7	0.3

For every 100 ha of arable land in Poland there are now approximately 21 vocationally active people. In the structure of forest use, those owned by the State Treasury and managed by the State Forests are still the most dominant group. At the end of 1994, they represented 78.5% of the national forest areas. Private forests represented 17.1% and gmina forests 0.9% of the total area of forests in Poland. Between 1991 and 1994, the percentage of forests managed by the State Forests decreased by 0.4%, while the percentage of privately owned forests increased by 0.1%.

Land consolidation and exchange works aiming at the transformation of certain physical structures are carried out on insignificantly small areas when the needs of such activities are considered to be necessary. Table 3 identifies and lists the volume of land consolidation and exchange activities that had been implemented between 1991 and 1994.

Table 3 The volume of land consolidation and exchange activities in Poland between 1991 and 1995

Year	Area in Hectares			Number	
	Consolidation	*Exchange*	*Total*	*Consolidated Areas*	*Participants in Consolidation*
1991	32,615	8,142	40,757	136	14,344
1992	19,759	7,844	27,603	184	8,475
1993	19,765	4,698	24,463	110	7,492
1994	12,664	3,980	16,644	90	4,635
1995	12,574	5,890	18,464	93	5,713
Total	97,377	30,554	122,931	613	40,659

Source: Data from the Ministry of Agriculture and Food Economy.

The consolidation works are carried mainly in the eastern and southern provinces of Rzeszów, Lublin, Białystok, Tarnobrzeg, Przemyśęl and Częstochowa.

Land in the Agricultural Property Resources of the State Treasury

The Agency for Agricultural Property of the State Treasury (AWRSP), established at the beginning of 1992, took over from the Agricultural

Property Resources of the State Treasury a number of assets. These included the assets of former State-owned farms, the National Land Fund, the State organisational bodies (which are not legal entities), and State-owned legal entities, etc. By the end of March 1996, the Agency had taken over, and had included within the Resources some 4,441,000 ha of land. This included 547,000 ha from the National Land Fund, approximately 3,752,000 ha of agricultural land, 78,000 ha of forests, 56,000 ha of forest and wooded land, 262,000 ha of lakes, 44,000 ha of ponds, 112,000 ha of waste land, and 114,000 ha of land occupied by buildings and transport facilities. Even so, over 250,000 ha of the land within the National Land Fund land had still not been included in the Resources. The largest areas of land taken over by the Resources were in the provinces of Olsztyn (398,000 ha), Szczecin (378,000 ha), and Koszalin (285,000 ha).

By the end of March 1996, the Agency had sold from the Resources various real properties with a total area of 283,000 ha (which represents only 6.4% of the area taken over). Of this, 229,000 ha consisted of land from the former State-owned farms and 47,000 ha of land from the former National Land Fund. As indicated by the analysis of structure of land sold, the average area of land covered by a single sales transaction was 6.9 ha. More than 8,400 ha (3.1%) was sold in lots of less than 1 ha, around 49,400 ha (18.3%) between 1 to 10 ha, 107,900 ha (39.9%) as lots between 10 and 100 ha and 104,600 ha (38,7%) were sold as real properties of at least 100 ha. The average price per hectare of land sold during the first quarter of 1996 was PLN 2003.00 and this was 34% higher than the average obtained during the whole of 1995 (PLN 1491.00/ha). The highest prices were obtained for real properties exceeding 100 ha (average PLN 2440.00 per hectare) and for the smallest lots of up to 1 ha (average PLN 1966.00/ha). The higher level of prices obtained during the auctions was influenced by the location of the lots close to or within the area of large urban areas, economic zones, etc., and these were sold for the highest amounts In the provinces of Szczecin and Warsaw, the prices per hectare of land exceeded PLN 5,000.00 while in provinces of Bielsko Biała, Katowice and Kraków, land was auctioned at PLN 4,000.00/ha. The lowest prices of PLN 1,000.00/ha were realised during auctions selling agricultural properties in the provinces of Konin, Koszalin, Krosno, Ostrołęka and Biała Podlaska.

The Agency sells real properties at auctions to both individuals and legal entities. The structure of the share to both groups of buyers (Table 4) indicates that the real properties of smaller size are of more interest to individuals, while the larger estates draw the attention of the legal entities. During the period ending 31st March 1996, the average area of estates purchased by the legal entities was 66 ha per contract, while in case of individuals it was 5 ha per contract.

Table 4 The area of land sold by the Agricultural Property Resources of the State Treasury according to area groups (in ha)

Province	By 31st March 1996			Of which during the 1st quarter of 1996		
	Total	*Of which*		*Total*	*Of which*	
		Individuals	*Legal entities*		*Individuals*	*Legal entities*
Area group in ha						
Up to 1.00	8,417	8,337	80	958	943	15
1.01 - 1.99	7,892	7,760	132	1,042	1,030	12
2.00 - 4.99	17,561	17,108	453	2,088	2,032	56
5.00 - 9.99	23,902	22,954	948	3,182	3,055	127
10.00 - 19.99	33,580	31,319	2,261	3,691	3,462	229
20.00 - 49.99	57,667	50,533	7,134	8,555	7,154	1,401
50.00 - 99.99	16,659	13,695	2,964	2,846	2,409	437
100.00 - 499.99	46,050	30,737	15,313	10,086	6,040	4,046
500.00 - 999.99	25,506	10,764	14,742	7,470	2,073	5,397
1,000.00 - I więcej	33,006	10,089	22,917	2,197	-	2,197
Total	**270,240**	**203,296**	**66,944**	**42,115**	**28,198**	**13,917**
Other Land*	12,556	X	X	1,375	X	X
Overall	**282,796**	**X**	**X**	**43,490**	**X**	**X**

* land occupied by buildings (also residential), separated objects, water bodies, etc.

Managing the land within the Agricultural Property Resources of the State Treasury, the Agency distributed (by the end of March 1996) land, free of charge, to the following entities:

- legal entities (churches) (20,546 ha);
- State Forests for afforestation (24,120 ha);
- gminas for the purposes of the performance of their tasks (5,432 ha);
- persons possessing perpetual usufruct rights to land (2,244 ha);
- others (5,142 ha).

By the end of March 1996, the Resources still possessed 4,092,000 ha of land of which the areas identified below were used and operated in the following ways:

- leased land (2,804,000 ha);
- administration purposes (333,000 ha);
- management purposes (39,000 ha);
- perpetual usufruct (8,000 ha);
- in State Treasury farms managed by temporary administrators (435,000 ha).

Additionally, the Resources included 472,000 ha of land that was not distributed or that was in use without a contract.

The most frequent method used by the Agency to manage the assets taken over for the Resources is through leasing. When faced with the common lack of capital in agriculture, the process of leasing requires lower capital investment than purchase. The process of leasing provides a convenient and relatively easily available method of making available to a wide circle of farmers and other business entities, suitable agricultural properties. By the end of March 1996, the Agency had entered into 149,00 leasing contracts for properties having a combined area of some 3,133,000 ha. As a result of expiring or terminating contracts, almost 330,000 ha of land, i.e. almost 10% of land that had originally been leased, was 'returned' to the Agency.

The analysis of leased land indicated that by 31st March 1996 lease contracts were signed for the real properties for the following area groups:

- up to 1 ha (1.3% of the total leased area, 48.2% of all leased contracts);

- 1-10 ha (5.9% of the total leased area, 40.1% of all lease contracts);
- 10-100 ha (12.3% of the total leased area, 8.6% of all lease contracts);
- over 100 ha (80.5% of the total leased area, 3.1% of all lease contracts.

The average area of real property leased from the Resources by individuals was 10 ha per contract, while in the case of real properties leased by legal entities it was almost 443 ha per contract. The average contractual lease period was 7 years (for the smallest lots this was 6 years, but for the real properties exceeding 100 ha, this was 11 years).

Plans concerning the physical management of rural area

The management of rural areas is conditioned by the major objectives concerning the directions of development. The management strategy is a consequence of the work needed to achieve such objectives. The direction that determines the objectives include:

- improvements in the use of human labour, natural resources and the means of securing the supplies of agricultural products and other goods, together with services adjusted to the demand of the domestic and international markets;
- modernisation of market and institutional links between rural areas and their surroundings aimed at improving the quality of the agricultural food products and increasing in incomes of the rural population;
- the development of multifunctional modes of area management;
- modernisation and development of the technical and social infrastructure in rural areas;
- protection of, and care for, the natural environment, historical heritage and landscape values.

Success in achieving these objectives will depend upon numerous conditions relative not only to agriculture but also to other areas of the economy. It will depend on the policy in financial, fiscal, social, food, ownership transformation, foreign trade areas, as well as scientific achievements and ecological conditions. This applies to both the level of a village, region, and to the entire country.

The development of a future image for rural areas and agriculture suffers as a consequence of looking at it from the perspective of its current status in Poland and its current status in the developed countries. This approach is not always appropriate, as the future status will be under influence from a variety of different factors. The answer to the question of 'where are we going?' depends on providing precise answers to two initial questions of 'where are we now' and 'where do we want to be?' While answering these questions the following aspects should also be considered:

- What supports the achievement of the objective and how can it be developed?
- What hinders the achievement of the objective and how can that influence be decreased?
- What should be rejected and what new elements should be introduced?

The current analyses and scientific studies indicate that the opportunities for the rural areas are linked to a 'balanced multifunctional development'. The model of economy in rural areas should depend on the status of the ecological and landscape conditions. These conditions should determine the profile of the economic and human activities in the rural areas. A thesis formulated in this manner will secure stability and the protection of the environment.

The first stage in implementation of the environmental model of the economy will result in the delimitation of rural areas, at different scales depending on the scope of the elaboration. As a result of that activity the following types of areas should be identified:

- those that are excluded from economic activities as a result of a high level of sensitivity to the environment, including areas of high natural values;

- those that have a limited level of freedom of economic activities where only certain selected forms of ecologically- oriented economic activities will be permitted;
- those with few limitations to economic use, which will include areas highly resistant to deterioration and with a high production potential.

The model of economy presented in this paper results from the principles of a balanced (ecological) development of rural areas. It satisfies the requirements of an ecologically sustainable development. In the balanced economy, rural areas must satisfy different functions (multifunctional development), assuming that production functions shall not be the dominating ones, although they may be important.

Agriculture and food economy will continue to be the major characteristics of the rural areas and, as a consequence, some details concerning their development will be described. The direction and type of agricultural production is the result of numerous factors: some resulting arising from the need to feed the population and others arising from the natural beauty of a region. The first group usually implies means by which production can be maximising. The second group of factors is more related to the development of numerous checks to ensure that the scenic values of the region are not degraded, which often means that intensification of farming has to be prevented. In agriculture, the final effect, i.e. its product and its suitability for consumption, are important. This should be a health safe product. Although already the initial assumption states that the task of the agriculture is production of safe food, independent of the type of farm, the influence of different types of farms upon the environment is not identical since the major objectives of the different types differ. The intensively farmed areas are oriented towards the production of health-safe food, while ecologically-friendly farms are more focused towards environmental protection linked, to production of super-safe food. As a consequence, the interests of nutrition and of environmental protection have to be reconciled, together with the interests of the producers, i.e. their income is also of major importance.

The starting point for a determination of the direction for the development of agriculture within a given area, is the acceptance of the need to develop all types of economic activities in agreement with the principles of ecology. Such an assumption gives priority to the environmental protection, while maximising the income of farmers, although important, is second amongst the environmental priorities.

The physical space of the different areas varies significantly and, as a result, also the development of new types of farms, particularly those oriented towards environmental protection, will have different perspectives. For instance, ecologically-friendly farms established within areas known to be polluted, will protect the environment but the products will not be safe. The same also applies to farms established in the lower sections of the water catchment areas, where the plants will be subject to the biogenes from the entire catchment. The function of such farms is sometimes limited to environmental protection only.

The answer to the question of what form of agriculture should be pursued means answering a number of issues, such as what structure of land use we should have, what types of production are required, etc. The baseline for ecological agriculture is the development of such a landscape structure that gives the right direction to the circulation of elements in the environment, thus preventing the accumulation of harmful compounds. Therefore, the important aspect is the structure of land use, which means indicating where, what type of land use and what relationship should be between them (in both area and physical terms) should be maintained. The rigors related to the operation of ecologically-friendly farms and the aspects of profitability allow that introduction of such farms, or even integrated farms over the entire region will be impossible. That is why it is possible to talk about the stages of the ecological conversion of agriculture or the level of ecologically-oriented agriculture. Based on the current analyses, two concepts of ecological conversion of agriculture could be proposed, using a system of protected areas, and using a combined system of social needs and agricultural, in combination with forms of ecological valuation. In both concepts, the environmental protection has the priority and the only difference is in the path to be followed in reaching the final objective.

The methodology behind the first concept, that of an ecological conversion of agriculture using a system of protected areas, is that initially all protected areas (of various nature) are established and that this will result in the necessity (it introduces constraints) and offers the opportunities for operating ecologically-oriented farming. The development of more or less ecologically-oriented farms is also linked at the form of protection. Therefore, within the more strictly protected areas (national parks, landscape

135

parks, etc.) only ecological farms should be developed, while within less strictly protected areas (areas of protected landscape) integrated farms should also be developed. This concept also assumes a gradual achievement of the objective. However, work in the existing protected areas, and in those areas that are planned for future protection, work should start immediately.

The nature of the second concept (using a combined system of social needs and agricultural, in combination with forms of ecological valuation) means searching for natural areas, which are open and predisposed to the implementation of ecological farms and also for those areas with a high level of social approval for the development of ecologically-friendly agriculture. Within the first area, the farmers should themselves find motivation for the transition towards ecologically-oriented farming (ecological education should assist this process), while in the other areas the farmers should turn to ecological agriculture out of moral and social duty. The areas which, because of their natural environment, are open and predisposed to the development of ecologically-oriented agriculture are those which can be identified for reasons of the ease of production of safe food, and the need to protect the high values of the natural environment (the values endangered in the case of the existence of other forms of agriculture).

Conclusion

The areas with a high level of social acceptance for the introduction of ecologically-oriented agriculture are, in general, those areas where it is easier to persuade the people and where it is easier to introduce the limitations related to ecologically-oriented agriculture. Such areas may be identified for the reasons of:

- natural factors in the form of the presence of protected areas, which means impact of certain limitations imposed for reasons which are not agriculture based, such as the presence of poor soils and the lack of tradition in operating intensive farms. For some people, it is easier to start something from scratch rather than attempting to shift to another type of production;

- social and economic factors such as the presence of areas with lower level of mechanised work and agricultural technology and the presence of a susceptible organisational structure.

References

AWRSP (Agency for Agricultural Property of the State Treasure), 1996. *Report from the Activities of AWRSP for the 1st Quarter,* Warsaw.

GUS (Central Office for Statistics), 1995. *Statistical Yearbook of the Provinces,* Warsaw.

GUS (Central Office for Statistics), 1995. *Environmental Protection,* Warsaw.

Would a registry map hang comfortably in a round mud hut? A register of titles for Zimbabwe's communal areas: philosophical and technical considerations

Mika-Petteri TÖRHÖNEN
Helsinki University of Technology, Department of Surveying, Espoo, Finland
David GOODWIN
University of Zimbabwe, Department of Surveying, Mount Pleasant, Harare, Zimbabwe

Abstract

This paper presents findings of a research project, which investigated the granting of title in Communal Areas in Zimbabwe. The research took place between May and June 1996, and, very broadly, it considered the problematic interaction between customary African land tenure, and modern land management systems.

The land issue is probably the most thorny with which the present Government of Zimbabwe has had to grapple in the sixteen post-independence years. This paper recognises the dilemmas and compromises inherent in granting individual titles in communal lands, it summarises and comments on recommendations made by the Land Tenure Commission, and it attempts to clarify options for Issuing a form of title in Communal Lands.

Introduction to the Communal Lands

The Communal Land tenure system in Zimbabwe includes three main components, namely arable, residential and common land. Under the Communal Lands Act (1981), communal land legally vests in the State, but families hold secure use rights, so that ownership effectively belongs to and is administered by tribes. Land is theoretically not alienable outside of the tribe. A residential parcel, or homestead, usually includes a domestic vegetable garden and fruit trees. Arable land may comprise one or more fields, sometimes widely separated, and sometimes with one or more members of the family having the exclusive use of a certain field or fields. Common land is held under communal tenure and is utilised for grazing and the gathering of firewood and other materials. Land is worked both by families living in the area, and by urban workers originating from the area.

The Communal Areas today cover 16.3 million hectares, which is 42% of the total land area in Zimbabwe. Although the soils in these areas are generally the least fertile in the country, 70-80% of Zimbabwe's population are concentrated here. It is estimated that there are over three times more people living in the Communal Lands than the environment can sustain (Zimbabwe, 1994), with proportionally excessive livestock levels.

History and statutory tenure

The Communal Areas land tenure of today derives from the customary tenure of the pre-colonial era, although it has evolved over the years. Rights are vested in groups, households, and individuals. Family rights have always been inheritable, and a type of subdivision allowed, and it is also possible to have residual rights to certain fallow land.

In the 1890s, when the English started to settle in Zimbabwe[1], the British government created native reserves, generally in areas that were considered unsuitable for the settlers[2]. It was a mammoth undertaking to transfer native Africans out of the areas reserved for the settlers, and took many years. The Land Apportionment Act of 1930 formalised the racial segregation of land. The statutory development relating to the communal areas included an attempt to individualise land tenure in 1951[3], but it faced mass resistance and had to be scrapped in 1961. In 1965[4] tribal land authorities were created in order to incorporate indigenous leaders to operate under District Commissioners. In 1969[5] the land area was divided into two, half for whites and half for blacks (Zimbabwe, 1994: vol 1, p. 10).

The independence struggle, which led to independence in 1980, called for radical land reform. Consequently, a new legal basis for land tenure in communal areas was created[6] by the incoming Government. The President became the formal landowner of all communal land, with Administration being done by the Ministry of Local Government, Rural and Urban Development and implemented through the Rural District

Councils[7]. The Councils were to supervise the use and allocation of land according to customary law. Two types of committee, the Village Development Committee (Vidco) and the Ward Development Committee (Wadco) were created after Independence to carry out grass roots administration. The idea behind the new statute was for local government to extend its jurisdiction to embrace farmland of all types, including communal land (Zimbabwe, 1994).

Present status

In order to meet the demand for cultivable land by the growing population, the government of Zimbabwe created a commission to carry out a comprehensive land tenure study in the country. The Land Tenure Commission[8], which published its report in 1994 (Zimbabwe, 1994), found that the administrative structure in communal land areas had largely collapsed, and statute was no longer followed. The official land administration had ignored customary tenure and had considered the rule of traditional chiefs over land illegal. Tensions had thus built up between the village committees and traditional leaders.

The main findings of the Land Tenure Commission of 1994 regarding communal lands are as follows:

- the land is still held under traditional freehold tenure giving ownership rights to families;
- traditional leaders are not recognised in statute, but in practice they are the land administrators;
- Vidcos are not democratically elected;
- traditional leaders' knowledge about and power over land is very much stronger than that of the official Vidcos and Wadcos;
- the confusion between official and unofficial authorities has resulted in violations in administration;
- the village demarcations decided by Vidcos are contradictory to those which traditional Kraalheads recognise;
- traditional tenure has been weakened by the status of all Communal Land changing to State Land, specifically in terms of land acquisition, compensation etc.

In conclusion, according to the Land Tenure Commission, it is clear that the overlapping interests between traditional and official local government is disturbing the land tenure in Communal Areas. It has caused a situation were rules are not followed and the power of authorities is perceived as confused. There is severe land pressure in communal areas, but there is no further land to allocate in order to alleviate this pressure. Subdivisions are very common due the rapid growth of population, and the holdings of many families are fragmented into a number of separate parcels. However, there are advantages as well as disadvantages in this, for example dispersed fields are considered a way of lowering the risks of failed crops. Consolidation[9] has been attempted in areas not considered ideal for farming, but it has been ineffectively executed[10]. Investment in immovable property has been very rare. Some public sector investments have taken place, for example irrigation schemes, but not on an adequate scale.

Fieldwork

The writers of this paper carried out comprehensive fieldwork on land tenure in the Communal Lands of Zimbabwe, during May - June 1996. The research team also included a Shona[11] speaking surveyor, who took care of interpretations both in terms of the Shona language and the Shona culture. The research included four different areas which were as diverse as possible. However Matabeleland[12] had to be omitted at this stage.

The first, and main, part of the fieldwork included field questionnaires and test cadastral surveys utilising GPS methods. The first phase of the research was conducted in the Makumbi village, close to Harare City (about 40 km distant). The research team stayed in a nearby Mission during the interview period, and again during the data-checking phase. The remainder of the fieldwork involved a number of villages in the Masvingo district, Sabi-valley and Nyanga district.

The Makumbi village typified a communal land in close contact with the capital. The Masvingo area, specifically Glenclova, represented a more remote communal area, generally less fertile and with a lower rainfall. The Sabi-valley was selected as a representative of one of the most degraded lowveldt areas in the country, with extremely low rainfall and highly degraded soil. Finally the Nyanga hills were deemed typical of a communal land in the Eastern Highlands with a very high rainfall and fertile soil.

142

A questionnaire was prepared in order to structure the discussion with interviewees. However, it was soon noticed that relevant issues could best be covered in thematic discussions, which roughly followed a few main areas of interest. This kind of approach enabled the discussions to advance in a direction that an interviewee considered important. The fieldwork results were generally unambiguous, but a few contradictory answers occurred, specifically concerning the 'official' administration set-up. This sort of ambiguity illustrates the problem only too well.

After the fieldwork, the results were discussed in separate interviews with officials from: the Ministry of Lands, the Ministry of Local Government, the Ministry of Agriculture, Agritex[13], Makumbi Mission, the Survey Institute of Zimbabwe, the Women's Resource Centre and finally with a Chief (Chasi (1996); Chinamura (1996); Chivore (1996); Mchena (1996); Musodza/Makombe (1996); Nduku (1996); von Nidda (1996) and Zhou (1996)). These interviews provided the necessary illumination of our research findings and also gave valuable scenarios about the future of land tenure in the Communal lands.

Fieldwork findings

Field discussions began with a general discussion about the land tenure in the Communal Areas and the viability of daily life. And responses were found to be very similar throughout. Families farming in the Communal Lands usually live on the land that they cultivate. Often some family members have moved to a town to work, or to seek work. In the areas close to towns, people also commute from their homesteads. Some years ago the family members that lived in a town used to bring back resources to their rural homes, but owing to escalating problems in towns, the position is now reversed, and in many cases the rural homes have to subsidise their town relatives. This is absurd since they can barely produce enough food for themselves. A minority of rural homes have good access to water, and are able to grow vegetables for town markets and earn a comparatively decent living. In Makumhi, which is close to Harare, land seemed to be quite well utilised, although some conservation problems occurred, always connected with water. In the Sabi-valley, in contrast, hardly anything was growing apart from crops on Government irrigation schemes. The team visited the areas after a very good rainy season, which had followed eight or so years of drought. It was sobering to realise that the kind of desperate, hopeless farming that we saw was about as good as things ever got.

The land tenure review did not provide many surprises. Land was usually handled as a family unit, usually with the father acting as a landowner. In case of the death of a father, either his widow or one of his sons inherit the landholdings. Normally all land in the communal lands is controlled by men. Women gain access to land only through their husbands or parents (the latter is often the case if a divorced woman returns to her parents' homestead). Women do not inherit land in cases where there are sons to inherit. A woman landholder, except by virtue of marriage, is always an exception. This is a burning issue in Zimbabwe, since there have been cases where widows have actually been evicted from their homes after the death of their husbands. The problems are most pronounced in cases of polygamous marriages, when a widow is not the principal heir's parent. The case is different if the marriage is registered under the Roman-Dutch law, but this is comparatively rare in the Communal Lands where most marriages still take place under customary law.

Family lands consist of fields, gardens, and residential parts. Most families possess only one parcel that is divided into many fields. However, some, perhaps the more influential families, seemed to have a few parcels in reserve. In cases where there are multiple wives, the number of residential areas in theory multiplies accordingly, but usually in practice this is no longer possible. The traditional avenue for gaining access to land is by marriage, when young men expect to be allocated their own farms from unallocated arable land in order to house and support their new families. However, except in very remote areas where the demand on land is low, this is often no longer possible since vacant, arable land rarely exists. In practice, a new family is given a share of the existing family land. The big question is whether a family parcel, and interests to it, are fragmented accordingly or whether the original land is dealt with as an undivided unit. And what emerged, is that the cultivated land is in fact usually fragmented into discrete fields for each family unit, but, with very few exceptions, the original family land is still considered as a single administrative unit. Our research team, somewhat to our surprise, was told wherever we went that family tenure in the communal lands is far from collapsing. We did notice, though, signs of stress on family tenure, for example different age and sex groups had rather different attitudes towards it. Young men who had been allocated a piece of family land usually considered it their own, while their parents would consider it family land.

Land administration was found to be very ambiguous, with a variety of executors without clearly defined roles. The village Kraalheads seemed to have the most real power. A village consists of several family homesteads. The Makumbi village, with 155 households, is considered a big village, while the Buwu village in Nyanga has only twenty households. Typically, a headman controls a group of close villages, and a Chief controls the whole district. The Chiefs power over land is rather blurred. It could perhaps best be described as a spiritual power which, however, should not be underestimated. Officially, no acquisition methods exist other than the allocation of non-allocated or idle land and inheritance. Improvements on land may be sold when land is vacated. Customarily a Kraalhead would have reallocated vacated land for no charge, other than perhaps a small customary tribute. But cash transactions have been occurring. The research team was told of cases where people had bought houses from a family that moved to town, and thereafter the Kraalhead had allocated the cultivated land associated with the house to the newcomer. What, then, was actually bought and what was sold? The house only; the arable land only; or the complete parcel together with its improvements? Putting this question another way around, who are the beneficiaries of what on the face of it seems to be a hidden land transaction, the original occupant or the Kraalhead? Previously unallocated land does not always appear to be apportioned equitably by the Kraalhead, and it would seem that when land is scarce a Kraalhead has been tempted to get the maximum benefit from these rare allocations. In some cases these allocations were referred to purely and simply as 'sales', because while a modest tribute is called for by tradition, some headmen seem to have abused this for their own enrichment. We met some bitter young men, who were getting desperate because they were anxious to get married, but could not do so, since the land was scarce and a price of the 'tribute' required for a new allocation was very high. Some renting had occurred, but, as with unofficial sales, amazingly few cases came to our notice. To sum this up, it can be stated that land in the Communal Areas of Zimbabwe is still not commoditised, at least, not on a significant scale.

The official administration structure involving the Village and the Ward Development Committees seemed to have little real influence. The Video and Wadco system has been criticised as being mainly a political tool designed to ensure support for the ruling party in rural areas. The Video chairman's role in land administration practise is unclear, although they themselves stress it when asked. The only function of the Wadco seemed to be to collect government dues, such as the dipping fee. All matters concerning the keeping of livestock and the land area possessed are in practice done by the Kraalheads, who seem to provide the link between the traditional and statutory administration. The District Administrator is the highest land official, but seems not to interfere with grassroots level administration. Agritex (the Department of Agricultural, Technical, and Extension Services) is charged with extension advice, and it generally plays a very active role, although this does appear to vary from place to place. An inherent weakness would seem to be that while Agritex can advise, it has no means of insisting that its' advice is followed. Agritex was reported to be taking part in new allocations, but it transpired that this was restricted to conservation and water management advice rather than issues of land administration. None of the above mentioned administrators' roles is clearly defined. In conclusion, there are clearly too many authorities to function effectively, and this has enabled the headmen to do basically what they want to, a situation that is open to violation and corruption.

Security of tenure through the granting of title was one of the main issues we wished to investigate, since it is always used as a major justification for agrarian reform. In the Communal Lands, it was found that land holdings are not perceived to be very secure, since all land belongs to the Government and it has been wielding its power openly enough to make people aware of this fact. For example, the possibility of a new game reserve may be a big threat if it is planned on ones valued cultivation. The compensation offered covers improvements on land, but ignores the loss of fields or residential land, which has in the past lead to individual tragedies. Political development has been unpredictable in so far as the land question goes, and peasants are extremely aware of this, which naturally detracts from their security. Insecure tenure has without doubt affected to some extent willingness to undertake long term improvements. Rural credit systems do not function well, if at all, and this reflects the security of tenure. However, remarkably, people seem not to be overly alarmed about compulsory acquisitions, and the danger of losing their rights to someone other than Government did not appear to be an issue at all. Having said this, one has to bear in mind that women do not have any rights at all, and if they do, these are very insecure compared with those enjoyed by men.

As mentioned above, rural credit systems presently seem not to be functioning, but we found that the desire for them is smaller than one might expect. Some credit systems existed until recently, mainly providing seeds and fertilisers against an easy payback programme. However, people reported a number of problems in paying the money back, and the system has vanished over the years. The Agricultural Finance Corporation (AFC) also issued loans in the past in rural areas, but rallying politicians had interfered with this by announcing that since it was Government's money, people need not pay it back, as it was actually theirs by right.

As well as large irrigation schemes, small private irrigation schemes occur fairly frequently in communal areas, specifically in gardens where valuable vegetables are grown for sale. Vegetable gardening is especially important in the areas close to large towns. However food cultivation still principally depends on rain-fed agriculture. Fertilisers seem to be commonly used, but precisely to what scale remains unclear. Housing development varies from very satisfactory huts of sun dried mud or bricks, and even cement-block houses in the more fertile/less remote areas, through to rather poor mud and pole huts in areas such as the Sabi-valley. Quite a number of wells and dams are built, usually by communities rather than individuals but in better off areas also by families. In the cases of private boreholes, the water is not denied to the whole community. River water is utilised, usually without limitations, or at least not to members of the village. This appears rather strange considering the huge importance of the water. We observed cultivation that was obviously situated far too close to a river, resulting in loss of topsoil and dam siltation.

Common land is used for firewood collection, common cultivation and hunting. Access is restricted to village members. Tracks and paths are also all considered to be in the public domain, at least to all villagers. So too is grazing on fallow land, although during the cropping season grazing is restricted to common land.

Boundary lines are in general remarkably clear, and it seems that they are almost never disputed, although some disputes were reported between one village and the next. We were told of one case where adjacent villages could not agree on their common boundary line and finally they had to take the case to the District Administrator (DA). The DA proved to be unsympathetic, and simply drew on the map a curious line which had absolutely nothing to do with the disputed case, and then terminated the proceedings abruptly, saying that the case was closed. Boundaries between families do not in general have accurate turning points, and boundary lines themselves have not been accurately determined. Each farmer can, however, point out the boundaries without hesitation. In one case, the farmer when asked by the research team to point out his boundaries, deputed a young boy, implying that the boy knew the boundaries just as well as he did himself, and there was no need to waste his own valuable time. Demarcation in past times was done by piling up stones in the parcel corners, very possibly a natural extension of the principle of possession by virtue of first clearing of land (Sorrenson, 1967), so that the stones cleared off arable land naturally become the boundary markers. The piles seem largely to have vanished by now, but earth banks, grass ridges created by ploughing and hoeing, and also paths which tend to skirt growing crops, appear to have taken over as evidence of the boundaries. The problem is that stones, although they are a natural way of marking turning points, are also useful for a great many other things, such as walling in cattle kraals and building houses, so they tend not to remain gathered together in one place for very long.

No land register, as such, exists for Communal Land, but certain information is collected and kept. For example Kraalheads usually maintain a list of households in their village, which is used by the District Councils for collecting different fees. Although some of these fees relate to the land held by families, the lists are purely descriptive, not graphical.

How would one notify people in the communal areas about an adjudication campaign, or that plans were being displayed for an appeal period? We included certain questions in our questionnaire in order to find a feasible way of contacting villagers. And what emerged was that the main media, as far as the communal lands of Zimbabwe are concerned, is radio, and specifically Channel Two, which provides programmemes in both major African languages. However, the best way to distribute messages within a village is probably still the traditional method involving the Kraalhead. Although there were minor differences from village to village, we found that all the Kraalheads are accustomed to, and have the means of reaching the whole village within a day or two, for example by messengers or 'shouting places'.

Peasants' thoughts about the future of the Communal Lands varied a great deal. Many interviewees expressed the wish that the Government would acquire more land from the commercial sector for new resettlement schemes to be reallocated to peasants. We usually ended our discussions by speculating about the possibility of title to Communal Land. For some people the idea was completely foreign, hut an amazing number understood the concept, probably because title exists in urban areas of Zimbabwe. Older people were afraid that if individual titles were granted the traditional leaders would lose their control over communities, which would lead to complete anarchy. Many people professed themselves willing to buy or lease land from others, but very few seemed prepared to sell or lease out their own land. The enhancement of security of tenure which Government guaranteed title would provide was approved unanimously. However, many people pointed out that during these undeniably tough times, family tenure ensured that everyone would at least have some place to stay and survive. It is a sort of 'basic needs', bottom line existence to fall back upon, and until such time as the State can offer comparable security, abandoning it could be viewed as about as prudent as chopping up the lifeboats on a ship as one approached the hurricane belt. Full commoditisation of land appears to pose a threat to many, starting from the weakest groups. Mortgaging possibilities were welcomed, but perhaps with some hesitation because of the risk of losing the land. On the other hand some people volunteered the opinion that those who failed to pay back loans did not deserve to own the precious land. At the top of any 'wish lists' for investment seemed to be water: bore holes, dams, and irrigation. It is understandable that the water issue in Zimbabwe is probably even more pressing than that of land.

The idea that land could be held jointly by a man and his wife, and in cases of divorce that compensation or subdivision would occur, was agreed by some women and disagreed by others, who did not want to challenge tradition. The idea was seen by men as a threat to family tenure which would lead ultimately to the fragmentation of Communal Lands into non-viable agricultural units. Men were also unwilling to subdivide land to give to a divorcee, because it was felt that their new wives would need land. Many women felt that the most important place to begin was for a more equal distribution of work and of the crops, which they grew.

Future considerations

Recommendations by the Land Tenure Commission for Communal Areas

Land tenure:

- communal land tenure should be maintained but security of tenure improved;
- the legal and administrative structures dealing with communal land should be revised and strengthened;
- customary law on land, i.e. traditional freehold tenure, should be formalised in statute;

- state land ownership of Communal Lands should be relinquished;
- key sets of rights in terms of inheritance, sub-division and compensation should be recorded in statute;
- management of grazing and other communally owned natural resources should be improved.

Legal institutions:

- the statutory law should be expanded to recognise customary law;
- the principle of traditional freehold rights should be maintained;
- compensation for improvements when a householder leaves the community should be formalised;
- rights should be vested in the heads of households, but restricted so that they cannot act without consulting their dependants.

Administrative institutions:

- the traditional village under the Kraalhead should be recognised;
- village members should have perpetual rights over the land and all resources in the village;
- a procedure should be established for maintaining and updating a permanent record of villagers;
- communities should have the right to select any new members;
- the Village Development Committee should be replaced with a traditional board[14];
- a Village assembly should be established having all villagers as members and the Kraalhead as Chairman[15];
- an avenue should be established to enable Village Assemblies to obtain technical advice on record keeping, etc., from the civil service;
- the administrative line from Kraalhead to Headman to Chief should be formalised and codified;
- a village assembly should be created, and integrated with the local court system;

- the entire Communal Lands should be surveyed, including an adjudication and survey of traditional village units, which should then be issued with Village Titles;
- arable and residential land units should be also be adjudicated and surveyed, and Land Registration Certificates issued for each household, which would then recognise and formalise the traditional customary rights of households;
- Villages' common land should be surveyed and a Land registration issued under the name of the village and held in trust by the Kraalhead;
- grazing rights should be left up to the villagers themselves to control;
- all transactions, sub-divisions, changes of ownership, inheritance, etc., should be recorded;
- the Communal Lands should have their status altered from State Land to Traditional Village land;
- some kind of development should take place for irrigation schemes.

Inheritance:

- family inheritance should continue, with spouses inheriting primarily, and in polygamous cases each wife retaining her land rights;
- the Village Assembly should act as a court of appeal in cases of dispute, specifically if a dependant ignores his/her duty towards other family members;
- the Village Assembly should protect the rights of widows;
- a Family trust should be established if both parents die.

Communal area reorganisation:

- the Communal area Reorganisation Programme should be revised and redirected;
- decisions concerning the Communal Lands should be decentralised.

Land rights for urban workers:

- urban workers should maintain their land rights on Communal Lands, at least until their position is much more secure;
- the Village Assembly should assess the relevance of the rights of each member;
- land acquisition for urban workers should be eased.

Investment and productivity:

- provision of infrastructure in the Communal Areas should be restored as a political priority in order to encourage more private investment in land;
- to revise the position of rural credit on the strength of a clearer administrative structure;
- the credit system should function on a village level, whereby a villager receiving a loan would be selected by and guaranteed by the Village Assembly.

Present situation and plans

As an outcome of the Land Tenure Commission's (LTC) recommendations, the former Ministry of Lands, Agriculture, and Water Development was split into two ministries: the Ministry of Lands, and the Ministry of Agriculture.

The Ministry of Lands has been specifically tasked with implementing the Commission's recommendations. Government has approved these recommendations, but they had not been officially discussed in Parliament by June 1996 (Muchena, 1994). At present the new Ministry is busy getting itself organised and seeking its final form, so the implementation of the LTC's recommendations may be said to have started by the creation of the administrative set-up. However, the Ministry considers the rest of the implementation to be an extremely difficult task (Musodza & Makombe, 1994).

The basic tenure reforms have been started by a planning phase, firstly of the administrative and secondly the legal reform. The Department of Lands and Technical Services has been established in the Ministry of Lands for the implementation of the actual work, but by June 1996 only two people had been nominated for a post in the department. The legislative reform preparation started with discussions by the Attorney General's office. Originally the idea was to draft a comprehensive land bill, but it was decided to start rather by revising the existing legislation. Presently various professionals that represent every facet of land tenure are being consulted. One of the principal ideas in Government is the establishment of a land taxation system. However, it would be mainly targeted at the land areas that are underdeveloped or even completely idle, and it is not therefore targeted initially at the Communal Lands.

When the Government agreed in principle to the Land Tenure Commission report, they thereby agreed to establish a village title system. According to the present scenario, a village would consist of around twenty households. This was criticised by a Ministry of Local Government official, who pointed out that it would firstly entrench the whole country's village structure, and secondly be too costly, since it was unclear where the money would come from for each of the new trustees' allowances that the new system would create (Chivore, 1996). The essential idea behind village title is to let the villagers decide certain issues for themselves. The present Communal Land Act and the Chiefs' and the Headman's acts would be amended accordingly, so that the present ambiguous land administration would be clarified. It would recognise the Kraalheads' position as actual land administrators. Land management decisions would be made in a Village Assembly where each villager would have a seat. All village boundaries would be demarcated and surveyed and a village title would be issued to the Kraalheads, following directly the recommendations of the Commission. Each arable and residential parcel would also be demarcated and a Land Registration Certificate for each family be given. The District Administrator would then keep the records of them and give out a copy for the families. A Ministry of Local Government official pointed out that very little consideration has been given to the cost of technical work (Chivore, 1996).

Contrary to the recommendations of the Commission, all land would remain State Land, and individuals would get only use rights to it. This difference may sound merely cosmetic, but there is an important matter of principle involved, and it is also important psychologically. The Government is interested in enabling banks to issue loans against the use rights, but so far the banks have declared that they would not give out any loans against the kind of certificate described. In the vision that the Government presently has, the land would remain strictly non-marketable, which is also a tougher attitude than the Commission recommended. Banks consider this unacceptable since they want to be able to sell a property to cover any unpaid debt. Apparently they do not consider the village guarantee system to be adequate. Knowing the hardship experienced in the Communal Lands, the banks' concern is understandable. In a poor rainy season it might well be that crops for an entire community fail. In conclusion, the Government on the one hand would like to make land mortgageable, but on the other would not accept it becoming marketable, and there appears to be no easy way of resolving this difference.

The Government claims to be trying to strengthen family tenure by recording existing rights in land. For the village title, each family would be listed under the family head's name. The position of women would not be dealt by the Ministry of Lands, but would be kept as a separate issue. The Zimbabwe Women's Resource Centre and Network, which is a donor-aided organisation, criticise the Government for skirting this difficult issue. They consider the land tenure and gender issue to be inseparable (Essof, 1996). In terms of women's rights, the Ministry of Justice has been planning amendments to the present inheritance law. Up to now families have been able to opt to follow customary law or Roman-Dutch law. The aim is now to unify these into a single Act, which makes spouse and children equal heirs of the head of the household (White Paper) (Musodza and Makombe, 1996). We also heard some doubts expressed concerning the actual motives behind the Land Tenure Commission work. Even Government employees suspected it to have been just a well-publicised campaign calculated to show that the Government had not forgotten the poor in the Communal Lands. Whether or not it ever leads to significant change remains to be seen.

Possible areas of improvement

Status quo

It is clear that the present form of land tenure in the Communal Lands of Zimbabwe hinders proper utilisation of land. There is inadequate security of tenure, leading to degradation of land, a chronic lack of investment and either under-utilisation or else over-utilisation of land resources. Consequently, a very significant part of the land area in Zimbabwe is in the hands of people who have no means of utilising it properly. Administrative stagnation, which in any case of improvement has to be the first issue to be dealt with, also permits certain people to benefit more than others, which leads to despair in certain sectors of the population. Having said this, one has also to consider its strengths, particularly its very important life-jacket function. Communal Land Tenure in Zimbabwe provides a social security system for all those born in the Communal Lands. Whatever happens in ones life, there is always a place to return to for a fresh start. Presently every Zimbabwean with family connections in the communal areas perceives this connection vividly. If communal land is commoditisised there is a danger that too big a share of the population, and their descendants to come, will be cut off from this traditional security system, at worst resulting in certain sectors of society living in hopeless poverty, with all its attendant social ills.

Title

Over half of the land area in Zimbabwe, including large and small scale commercial farms and urban areas, presently enjoy freehold tenure. The formal title registration system, although not state guaranteed, offers secure tenure which increases the care and utilisation of land and most importantly enables the introduction of credit systems. Inevitably, it also leads to better utilised land. As far as developing countries go, it is a fairly well functioning system, and there would be obvious benefits in integrating the Communal Lands into the same system, or else developing a parallel system with cross-links. But there are inherent difficulties, and dangers. Firstly those living in the Communal lands are still largely small subsistence farmers, not fully integrated into the cash economy, and secondly if family land were to be commoditised, its sale at market value would arguably not compensate for the loss of what has above been termed its life-jacket function. Before embracing such a system, there would have to be means by which the Government could deal with a new, landless population.

Village title

The Land Tenure Commission recommended less radical action than the introduction of full, individualised tenure, namely a system of village title. The idea was to decrease the Government's direct administration of land, and to devolve certain powers to villagers. On the face of it this appears commendable, since it would codify and strengthen existing Communal Land Tenure practices. The only question is whether it would provide secure enough tenure to enable the full benefits of title registration to be realised. Recognition by the official credit system is essential. The village guarantee system makes sense, but one questions whether it would work in a society that is largely not yet integrated into the cash economy. These things have to be clarified, otherwise any changes made would be wasted effort. Whatever system is to be created, a new and different kind of stagnation should be avoided. Land Tenure in the Communal Lands is undoubtedly facing pressures for transition. A suitable system for today may not be the optimum system for tomorrow, and a system for a remote village may not be appropriate for a village on the outskirts of an expanding city. A system which disallows commoditisation of land should include the means for upgrading it to permit sale and lease, and ultimately full title, when this is found necessary democratically. Whatever development direction is selected, clearly defined administration is crucial, because if the structure remains as confusing as it is at present, no system will help the peasants, since the only real power is that of the strong over the weak.

Technical considerations

Initial assumption

There is little doubt that if Zimbabwe's cadastral system in its present form were to be extended to the Communal areas, it would not cope with the volume of new parcels added. On the other hand, if Government granted title to all holders of land rights, without any attempt to adjudicate rights or survey their extent, then there would be limited benefits either to Government or to the new owners, and in the long run as land changed hands there would be escalating confusion.

This paper therefore works on the assumption that, however approximately it is done, the following two things are necessary to the granting of title:

- firstly, some form of adjudication to ascertain what rights belong to whom. This step is necessary before tax may be levied, before orderly development may go ahead, before common land can be managed effectively, and before any reorganisation of land may take place; and

- secondly, some sort of picture or diagram needs to be created which shows the approximate shape of land parcels, and their positions relative to each other. Even if this is a very simple picture, it would assist in planning, and provide a vehicle on which to attach attributes such as taxable value, owners etc. Where one or both of these steps have been omitted, serious difficulties have ensued, for example in Malaysia.

For both situations, it is assumed that at least one visit will be needed to each land parcel, to ascertain what rights exist and to perform some sort of survey or field verification. Ideally, if a surveyor is attached to the adjudication team, the graphical picture can be built up at the same time as rights in land are ascertained. The LTC report recommended a 'grassroots' surveyor, on the adjudication team, with minimal qualifications, but supervised and checked at a higher level by a licensed surveyor.

Context: the past

The Land Tenure Commission (LTC) report found that the surveying of communal land parcels, and village boundaries was technically possible. Having considered a number of options, the method recommended was a digital monoplotting solution from GPS controlled aerial photographs and using digitisers and PC's. The task would be enormous, and it was estimated that it would take about twenty years to complete, and would cost about 130 Million US dollars with an estimated cost recovery period of ten years. The following list contain the main features and principles of the method:

- in general only one visit per parcel, at the time of adjudication, by a low grade surveyor who is part of the adjudication team;
- a subsequent visit by a better qualified surveyor only to a handful of points in an area, to co-ordinate any points, which proved not to be air visible and to fix control for the photogrammetry (enough control would be put in to permit a rigorous solution if it was needed in future);
- community participation in building airmarks at turning points in boundaries to engender commitment and work against a

handout mentality. This would also fulfil the need for a public ceremony to advertise where boundaries were;

- accuracies of about 2 metres relative accuracy, and 25 - 30 metres absolute accuracy, but capable of being done with simple equipment (digitiser and PC). The simple equipment would keep prices down, and also, since no surveyor would be disqualified from undertaking the work on the grounds of capital cost one could expect healthy competition;
- the initial accuracy would be upgradable at any time by rigorous photogrammetry with a stereoplotter to an order of about a hundred times better (10 - 20 cm absolute accuracy) in the case of disputes arising or if land values increased sharply;
- surveys all to be on the national grid system;
- public access to the land register;
- work to be done by the private sector, but on an open tendering basis and with the Department of the Surveyor General tasked with setting standards and quality checking work submitted before inclusion in a national, Land Information System (LIS);
- approximation of curvilinear boundaries in the field (eg. grass ridges or paths) by a series of straight line boundaries with marked turning points in order to come up with a comparatively small data set of vector information, which was independent of topographical mapping and which could be used as it stood for legal and fiscal purposes but which could also he overlaid as and when the need arose on a variety of topographical base maps (rectified photographs, line maps, rectified satellite imagery);
- a period of appeal before issuing title deeds;
- not trying to reorganise communal land simultaneously with adjudication but to do this as a separate exercise at a later stage as and when necessary.

The present

Most of the principles outlined in the Land Tenure Report (published in 1995) still hold good, but technology has not remained static. Differential, handheld GPS measurements (DGPS) are now possible. The Department of Surveying at the University of Zimbabwe now has a community base station which permits absolute accuracies of 2-5 metres with handheld GPS receivers up to several hundred kilometres away. The authors undertook some limited fieldwork to test the viability of this new technology for communal land boundary determination. The main issues were seen to be as follows:

- whether the 120 or so observations called for by the manufacturers was strictly necessary for the accuracy we required, or whether fewer measurements would be sufficient. If a smaller number of measurements were to be taken, they would take less time, the batteries would last for more observations at other points, and the data set collected would be smaller;

- whether measurements were possible close to or under trees;

- whether measurements were possible by surveyors with little specialised training, and whether a *data dictionary* could be designed to lead such a surveyor through a series of measurements without the possibility of mistakes and without forgetting to record any vital information;

- whether it was relatively easy to identify boundaries on photographs, and whether the photographs meant anything to the peasants;

- whether it was easy to simplify curvilinear boundaries in the field to a series of straight lines (see later); and

- what the cost implications were.

A data dictionary was designed before the first fieldwork phase, and modified on the basis of experiences in the field. Different numbers of measurements were taken at each point measured in the field: 10, 30, 60, and 120 measurements. Co-ordinates used to control these measurements were made by theodolites and EDM on the National trigonometric system, with accuracies of a few centimetres. This control was considered absolute for the purposes of our comparisons. The base station at the Department of Surveying, University of Zimbabwe was fixed in the same manner. A handheld TRIMBLE Geoexplorer receiver was used, but it was ascertained that Garmin and Magellan manufacturers offer comparable accuracies for a similar cost.

Trees were not found to present a problem. Many of the measurements were taken near to trees, and one fix was made right under the thickest tree canopy we could find, and no difficulties were experienced. From this point of view, the method is superior to photogrammetry, even rigorous photogrammetry using a stereoplotter.

Sets of four, penlight (AA) batteries were used in the Geoexplorer. A set lasted for about four hours, which becomes expensive, so one or more external, rechargeable battery packs need to be budgeted in for each receiver.

It was felt that more comprehensive tests would be needed at a later date to confirm the rule of thumb that about a metre in accuracy is lost for every hundred kilometres from the base station.

Beacons and boundaries

We found that the existing boundary system in communal areas is most often one of mutually agreed curvilinear boundaries, or in other words boundaries with a physical existence, such as grass strips, earth banks, paths and watercourses, which abutting owners recognise as their common boundary. No difficulties were experienced walking around these boundaries, but further work is needed in the lowveldt where there is a much lower rainfall and there are some boundaries with no physical demarcators. For reasons gone into below, it was felt that although boundaries should be left in the same place, they ought to be delineated in a simplified form by a series of straight lines approximating the boundaries. It was found in the field that it was quite simple to decide on which straight lines best represented a simplified boundary. Provided that a curvilinear boundary is agreed to in the first place by abutting owners, then no difficulties are anticipated in reaching consensus on the simplification of this boundary by a series of straight lines.

The question of whether turning points should be marked or not is debatable. The authors recommend that where there is a path intersection, or a corner in a grass ridge or some physical feature which people agree to, then this should simply be described, and nothing further needs to be placed. But where no physical evidence exists, which is sometimes the case, then drill holes in rock or else iron pegs with cairns of stones are possibilities for marking turning points. Nothing, of course, compares with a drill hole in rock for permanence, but where this is not possible, then iron pegs are probably the next best alternative. They are inexpensive, quite tricky to remove, and have only limited intrinsic and cash value, so it is not thought that theft would be a problem. Where markers were deemed necessary, they could be supported by descriptions such as, '12mm drill hole in rock 3.4 metres SE of wild fig tree'. We recommend that at the same time as the survey is done, the position of beacons be pricked on enlarged photographs or photomaps, and boundaries sketched in, land parcels labelled etc. This would firstly provide a check on the GPS measurements, but even more importantly it would show nodes and polygons, to make the topology completely unambiguous. These annotated photos could be archived for future reference, and even used at a later stage for rigorous photogrammetric mapping, since there would be an abundance of identified, pricked and surveyed ground control points. If a rectified photomap was used, then a copy could possibly be kept at village level for reference purposes.

It is felt that no matter what survey is done, and what monumentation is placed, the existing boundary system will be perpetuated, in that people will continue to recognise grass ridges or paths or piles of stones as their common boundaries. The point or line agreed to on the ground as a beacon or boundary is completely accurate, at a one-to-one scale. However, the essence of a graphical cadastre is that boundaries may be co-ordinated, and depicted on a plan to a far lower order of accuracy, and still be useful for a variety of purposes (see below).

So if beacons and boundaries are in general accepted in the field, then what difference would a survey make? The differences would be twofold:

- firstly, a graphical picture of the boundaries would then have been created, or at least an approximation of them by a series of straight lines, and this graphical record could potentially be used for such tasks such as planning, administration, taxation, mortgaging, transfer and lease of land, and appending attributes such as ownership information; and
- secondly, if any doubt or dispute arose, boundaries could be re-established, not simply by human memory, but by measurement.

Other than these, the system to the peasant would look the same. He would not have to change his idea of what a boundary was, and his rights would for all intents and purposes end and his neighbours' rights begin where they always had done. The difference would be in the new options available to the title-holder (subject of course to Government policy), and in the new possibilities open to Government.

Another obvious question, is that if the grass ridge or earth bank or path which is mutually agreed as the boundary was still accepted on the ground to be the effective boundary even after survey, then should it not be the boundary, and be mapped exactly as it is, without simplifying it to a series of straight lines?

The answer really hinges upon how one decides to delineate boundary information, or in other words what graphical record one keeps of boundaries. There are two main options. The first is to keep a large-scale topographical map or photomap of boundary features. The second option is to separate boundary information completely from topographical information. And there are pros and cons to each of these options, and a photomap is probably the easiest thing to comprehend to the rural farmer. But on the other hand a simplified vector map on the national trig system is more portable, in that one could easily overlay boundaries on any map or image at any scale. To overlay a purely graphical depiction of boundaries, for example from a photomap, onto a map or image at a different scale one would have to change the scale photographically or mechanically, or else digitise and alter the scale digitally. And if one did the latter, the points that one selected to digitise while sitting in an office or laboratory could never be as good as those actually decided on in the field with all interested landholders present.

On balance it is felt by the authors that something valuable would be added if consensus was reached in the field at the time of adjudication on a simplified series of straight lines which adequately represented curvilinear boundaries. In other words the boundary would stay the same, but its delineation would be simplified in such a way that there was no material gain or loss to any interested party. There would be comparatively few surveyed points, and a resultingly small data set, so that storage of co-ordinates, and maintenance and manipulation of data for various tasks would be quick and simple. And in a less developed country (LDC), simplicity counts for a great deal. The LTC report recommended an institutional structure where each district (53 in all) held a PC, with a non-graphics database and hardcopy General Plans of villages. Villages would also hold copies of General Plans. PC's are now freely available in the country, and repair facilities exist, and although it was felt that computer graphics should certainly not be linked in at this stage, textual information is a comparatively simple matter.

For any specific development project the responsibility would be on those funding the project to produce any topographic mapping which they required. Juridical information could be overlaid, and the millstone of maintaining and updating a large-scale topographical map or photomap would be avoided.

Another reason for delineating boundaries with straight lines, is that not all boundaries have a physical existence. The Thailand experience was that 80% of boundaries showed up from the air, and the remaining 20% had to be surveyed by ground methods (Angus-Leppan and Williamson, 1983). Looking at photographs of Thailand, this figure might even be higher in denuded areas of Zimbabwe. Undemarcated boundaries would, in the course of adjudication, be pointed out as a series of straight lines and turning points, and it would be far more efficient if these could be mapped immediately in the same way as the rest of the boundaries, rather than waiting for a field team to come in at a later stage and try to find the marks, which had been agreed to on the ground by the adjudicators, survey them and plot them on the photomap. Such a survey team would be moving at a different pace to the adjudicators, so if they came later it would mean more resources, more organisation and more things to go wrong. One ideally needs all surveys to take place while the adjudication is being done, and DGPS has now provided us with the enabling technology.

What happens if a boundary disappears, for example if a grass ridge is ploughed over, or a path falls into disuse? In such cases one could replace a boundary either by scaling from a topographic map or a photomap, or else by recourse to co-ordinates if one held those, or else by a combination of both. It must be stressed that relocation will never be necessary for the vast majority of boundaries, but mechanisms for replacing boundaries must be in place for the cases where it does become necessary. The present Roman-Dutch law in Zimbabwe recognises that the survey evidence and any written or graphical description may be ambiguous, approximate or incorrect, and rules that the most weight should attach to the position of the boundary as originally agreed to in the field as well as this can be re-established. Enduring, visible beaconing, regardless of type is therefore very important. Having said that, if physical demarcators are lost or removed, be they pegs or grass ridges, and their original position has to be re-established, or even just in confirming that markers are the original ones in substantially the same position, survey evidence may be crucial.

Acquisitive prescription (i.e. adverse possession) would still apply, so that if a boundary feature moved over time the position of the boundary would move with it, but perhaps the present period of thirty years should be reviewed for communal areas.

So in short, we recommend that boundaries remain as they are, but that they are delineated by a simplified series of straight lines which at the time of adjudication, are made to approximate the curvilinear boundaries accepted in the field. We recommend that these boundaries be held as a digital, data set which is completely separate from any topographic maps or rectified photographs but which may be overlaid as and when necessary.

Cost of the exercise

If one accepts that adjudication must take place regardless, then if the survey is done at the same time it would represent only a small additional cost. A GPS receiver would be needed with external rechargeable batteries, enlarged photographs for labelling and pricking (probably existing blanket photography could be enlarged without re-flying), several base stations to move around the country in support of groups of adjudication teams, and portable computers for downloading to at night to ensure that there had been no problems with the day's data collection. A handheld GPS receiver capable of recording data rather than just points (this is necessary for post-processing with data collected at the base station) is about US$ 3,000, with an additional US$ 375 for an external battery pack.

The LTC report also noted that one could kill more birds with the same stone, and thereby if the costs of the exercise could be co-ordinated with, for example surveys of wells and boreholes for one Ministry, or dip tanks for another, the overall costs could effectively be subsidised.

Accuracies

The fieldwork undertaken by the research team confirmed the 2-5 metre absolute accuracies quoted by the manufacturers. Quite a number of nearby points (about 15 km away from the base station) were in fact correct to below a metre. Comparing means of the groups of 10, 30, 60, and 120 observations, the results obtained are illustrated in Table 1.

Of note was the fact that there were normally less than 10 outliers in 220 observations, and that the widest separation between groups of observations was 4.2 metres, with the average being less than 2.5 metres. From this we concluded that 10 - 20 observations is probably sufficient to notice the presence of outliers, and give accuracies in the region of 5 metres. Relative accuracies are very likely to be better than 5 metres, but further tests are needed to confirm this. (Note: observations were taken at intervals of 5 seconds, i.e. 10 observations would take less than a minute, and 20 slightly over a minute and a half. This should not slow down the adjudication team appreciably.)

An advance party would really need to co-ordinate a point for a base station in a protected place with good visibility, a power supply, and where a computer could be locked up safely.

With respect to the data dictionary, it was found after initial tests that it was better to record points rather than area features. A description of a boundary turning point is necessary, and ideally the numbers of the land parcels to which it is common, and whether it is also part of a village boundary. The creation of the directory was found to be relatively simple, and it was easy to use thereafter even by a surveyor with very little previous experience.

Table 1 Comparison of the groups of GPS observations

Point number	Limit of all 220 observations other than the outliers (metres)	Number of outliers outside those limits	Limit of all observations including outliers (metres)	Widest separation between groups of readings (eg. 10 from 20) (metres)
1	2.5 * 1.4	0	N/A	1.0 (10-30)
2	7.5 * 2.5	5	8 * 5	4.2 (10-30)
3	3.8 * 1.3	0	N/A	2.5 (10 - 120)
4	2.0 * 1.0	3	2.5 * 2.6	1.0 (60 - 120)
5	4.2 * 0.9	4	4.7 * 0.9	3.9 (10 - 120)
(Note: all except 14 within 2.5 * 0.9)				
6	3.7 * 1.0	0	N/A	3.2 (10 * 120)
7	2.4 * 1.6	6	4.5 * 2.4	1.2 (10 - 30)
8	1.6 * 1.0	9	5.8 * 4.2	1.0 (10 - 120)
9	3.2 * 1.3	0	N/A	2.8 (10 - 120)
10	3.9 * 0.7	0	N/A	3.5 (10 - 120)

Summary and conclusions

Present situation in Communal Lands

The Communal Land tenure system in Zimbabwe includes three main components, namely arable, residential and common land. Irrigation schemes occur fairly frequently but food cultivation principally depends on rain-fed agriculture. Communal land legally vests in the State, but secure use rights are held by families, so that ownership effectively belongs to and is administered by tribes. The overall situation and life in the Communal Lands is not favourable, as there are over three times more people than the environment can sustain, with proportionally excessive livestock levels. There is no further land to allocate in order to alleviate the severe, land pressure.

The land tenure in the Communal Lands is remarkably homogenous. Families usually live on the land that they cultivate. Owing to extremely hard times in Zimbabwe, in many cases the rural homes have to subsidise their town relatives even though they can hardly keep themselves. Land is usually handled as a family unit, with the father acting as a landowner. Women gain access to land only through their husbands or parents and they do not inherit land in cases where there are sons to inherit. Family lands consist of fields, gardens, and residential parts. The traditional avenue for gaining access to land is by marriage, when young men expect to be allocated their own farms from unallocated arable land in order to house and support their new families. In practice, a new family is given a share of the existing family land, since vacant cultivable land is so rare. Other resources such as water are usually communally held and distributed. Tracks and paths are all considered to be in the public domain. During the cropping season grazing is restricted to common land only. Boundary lines are in general remarkably clear, and it seems that they are almost never disputed.

Land administration is very ambiguous, with a variety of executors without clearly defined roles. The village Kraalheads seem to have the most real power. The official administration structure involving the Village and the Ward Development Committees has little real influence. There are clearly too many authorities to function effectively, and this has enabled the headmen to do much as they please, a situation open to violation and corruption. In result the land holdings are not perceived to be very secure and it has without doubt affected to for example willingness to undertake

166

long-term improvements. Also the rural credit systems are not functioning at present.

Technical conclusions

There is technically no reason why communal land parcel boundaries could not be surveyed either on an individual plot level or a village boundary level. In the light of recent technological advances it is thought that 10-20 handheld DGPS measurements are probably the best way for the survey to be done at present, although things are changing the whole time. Survey should be done at the time of adjudication and using comparatively low grade surveying personnel guided by prompts in a suitably designed data dictionary.

The result would be a digital map with co-ordinates on the national grid system depicting straight line boundaries which approximated the curvilinear boundaries which were recognised in the field. This could be easily updated when changes occurred, and could also be overlaid very easily on any rectified map, photograph, or image.

A simple and secure mechanism would then exist which would encourage proper utilisation of land and which could be used for taxation, planning, borrowing using land as collateral, and the sale and leasing of land (subject to any controls, which are imposed by Government).

Neither does the adjudication of Communal Lands seem to be a particularly difficult task, apart from its scale. The key question is whether community participation can be obtained, and it would seem that this can be assured by involving the traditional leadership in the process. Village boundaries can be agreed by abutting leaders, although some disputes may arise. The peasants in the Communal Lands can quite easily be contacted via the existing traditional leadership, land holders can be determined easily as they or their relatives usually live on their holdings, ownership is seldom disputed, and boundaries are normally not subject to dispute, and in most but not all instances demarcation is clear.

Future considerations

There is little doubt that the beneficiaries of organised tenure system would include Government and the wealthy. But it is still far from clear how exactly changing this system would benefit the poor and those not completely integrated with the cash economy of the country, especially if communal land kept its status as State land and the holders of title were not able to buy, sell or lease land or raise a mortgage on it. On the contrary, land holders could immediately be taxed, and there is little doubt would be taxed, if for no other purpose than to meet the running costs of the new system. The present titles system in the Communal Areas has one overwhelming advantage, and that is that it costs almost nothing to run. However, the existing situation is unsatisfactory as people struggle with very basic survival.

What about if Government policy had changed and land had became fully commoditised? The Title system would serve many well but would also endanger the weak, who are the most vulnerable. If speculation in land was not rigidly controlled, then the system would enable families efficiently and irrevocably to lose their birthrights to the rich for the proverbial mess of pottage. It cannot be too strongly emphasised that communal land is the basic needs provision for about 80% of Zimbabwe's poorest people. If this provision were lost where would these people go? And what would they do in order to stay alive? And the answer is that they would go to the large cities to congest the roads and sewers, deplete the water reservoirs, and fleece the wealthy, sooner or later with recourse to violence.

A Village Title system would be a good compromise, but might not provide security strong enough to gain many of the benefits of a title system. It is quite possible that more good would be done by leaving family land substantially as it is, with some modifications, for example to give women, including widows, more recognition in law for their pivotal role in the family, to provide Government or donor guaranteed village loans for bore holes and small dams, and to set up peer pressure, micro-finance schemes along the lines of the Grameen model of Bangladesh.

In the end, there is probably no all-embracing solution for the land tenure system of the Communal Lands. In the future there could well be a variety of tenure systems providing various levels of title including the means for upgrading when found necessary democratically. Perhaps the most salient conclusion is that whatever line is taken, the recognition and codifying of the traditional leadership into statute is essential. Perpetuating the existing confusion could ultimately prove to be suffocating.

References

Angus-Leppan & Williamson, 1983. *Land and Titles in Thailand,* Department of Lands, Bangkok, Thailand.

Chasi Mutsa, 1996. Chief Agricultural Officer, Agritex. Interview at Agritex 4 June 1996.

Chinamura, Chief, 1996. Interview at his homeyard in the Makumbi village.

Chivore, Mrs. 1996. Under Secretary of the Ministry of Local Government, Interview at the Ministry, 17 June 1996.

Essof, S., 1996. Research Advocacy. Interview at the Zimbabwe Women's Resource Centre aid Network in 5 June 1996, Harare.

Muchena, O., 1996. Deputy Minister of Agriculture. Interview at the Ministry of Agriculture, 18 June 1996.

Musodza & Makombe, 1996. Principal Executive Officer (Mr. Musodza) and Acting Under Secretary (Mr. Makombe), of the Ministry of Lands. Interview at the Ministry, 11 June 1996.

Nduku, Mr. 1996. Land use planner at the Chinoi Agritex. Interview in 7 June 1996 at the Chinoi Agritex.

Sorrenson, M.P.K , 1967. *Land Reform in the Kikuyu Country,* OUP, London.

von Nidda, R., 1996. A catholic priest and missionary. Interview at the Makumbi Mission, 14 June 1996.

White Paper. *White Paper on Marriage and Inheritance in Zimbabwe.* Printed by the Government Printer, Harare, Zimbabwe.

Zhou, S., 1996. Private Land Surveyor, Head of the Survey Institute of Zimbabwe. Interview at his office on 13 June 1996.

Zimbabwe, 1994. Mandivamba Rukuni (Chairman). *Report of the Commission of Inquiry into Appropriate Agricultural Land Tenure Systems,* Volumes 1-3, The Republic of Zimbabwe, Harare, 1994.

Endnotes

[1] 1889 The Lippert Concession enabled white settlers to acquire lands from natives.

[2] 1898 Natives Reserves Order in Council.

[3] The Native Land Husbandry Act (NLHA).

[4] The Tribal Trust Land Act of 1965.

[5] Land Tenure Act.

[6] The Communal Land Act of 1981.

[7] The Rural District Councils Act of 1988.

[8] Commission of Enquiry into Appropriate Agriculture Land Tenure Systems 1993.

[9] Sometimes known as Communal Land reorganisation.

[10] Communal Development Plan of 1986.

---

[11] The biggest tribe in Zimbabwe, originating from the Bantu people.
[12] Home of the Ndebele, which originate from the Zulu of South Africa.
[13] Department of Agriculture, Technical and Extension Services.
[14] A Shona traditional board, *Dare* or a Sindebele traditional board, *Inkundla.*
[15] In Shona *Musha* or in Sindebele *Izakhamizi.*

Index